MAIN THING SERIES

NEVER THE SAME

DISCIPLE'S

JOURNAL

ON

KNOWING

GOD

JEFF KINLEY

David C. Cook Church Ministries—Resources
A division of Cook Communications Ministries
Colorado Springs, CO/Paris, Ontario

GREAT GROUPS
The Main Thing Series
Never the Same Journal
© 1994 Cook Communications Ministries

Cook Ministry Resources
a division of Cook Communications Ministries
4050 Lee Vance View, Colorado Springs, CO 80918-7100
www.cookministries.com

Edited by Sharon Stultz and Mark Syswerda
Cover and interior design: Jeff Sharpton, PAZ Design Group
Cover illustration: Paula Becker
Printed in U.S.A.

ISBN: 0-7814-5110-8
12-99

TABLE OF Contents

DEDICATION

To Dr. Steven J. Lawson
—my teacher, mentor, and friend—
who, more than anyone,
has forever impacted my life and ministry.

II Timothy 2:2

INTRODUCTION

Dear Friend,

Years ago, a friend of mine gave me the greatest challenge of all—to get to know God. I took that challenge, and my life was *never the same.*

I want this book to do the same for you! It's a book for young people who want to know God—not just to know about Him, but to know Him—personally, intimately, and deeply. It's a book that brings you face to face with who God is, what He has done for you, and how you can serve Him. In it, you'll explore what it means to be a disciple who experiences God as your Father, Jesus as your Savior, and the Holy Spirit as your Guide.

In short, you'll end up "getting more of God" in your life as He gets more of you. And by the time you're finished with this book, you will know God better than ever.

So take the challenge. Buckle up your spiritual seat belt and prepare yourself to be *Never the Same!*

Jeff Kinley

How to Use This Bible Study

To get started you will need a Bible, this disciple's journal, a pencil, and if you'd like, a notebook.

To begin with you will find that there is usually an intriguing activity or story to spark your interest in completing this Bible study. Have fun with it but don't stop there because you will make some exciting discoveries about your relationship with God when you keep going.

You will find that some, but not all, of the Scripture verses are printed here for you. We try to print out the Scripture whenever you are asked to mark it up by underlining, circling words, etc. However, we strongly encourage you to use your own Bible as you work through these studies. We use the New International Version and you should too, if possible. But don't worry, use whatever translation you are most comfortable with.

There is space for you to write down responses to the questions. If you find that you want more room to express yourself, write additional thoughts in some kind of notebook that will be easy to tote with you to the group Bible study. Make sure your notations are complete enough to make sense to you during the small group Bible study time. You may want to write down key words to spark your memory or you may need to write out complete thoughts—whichever works best for you.

There is also room to express yourself on the "Pray About It" page. Write out your personal conversations with God. Talk to Him about, well, anything. Keep track of your requests and God's answers.

Whatever you do, always try to complete the entire week's study before your small group meeting, so that you can get the most out of other people's comments. This way, you won't miss out by trying to catch up on your reading during the small group time.

UNIT One

God the Father

So you want to grow closer to God, huh? That's great, but it's going to take some commitment on your part.

You see, He's more than we can comprehend. He's the Triune God—Three in One. He's God the Father, yet He's also God the Son—Jesus, and He's God the Holy Spirit.

Anyway, let's start you out with God the Father.

You'll get a chance to dig into areas such as His existence since—well, since forever! You'll be awed by His power and His sovereignty, while being blown away by just a glimpse of His holiness! And you'll finish up by resting in the safety and security of His love.

So prepare to grow closer to God, and be prepared to learn that although none of us are deserving of His awesome love, He loves us anyway!

WEEK 1 — Alive and Well!

The Existence of God

Nietzsche
is dead—
God

God
is dead—
Nietzsche

1 Writing on the Wall

In the late 1800's, the famous German philosopher and atheist Friedrich Nietzsche declared to the world, "God is dead!" Though raised in a Lutheran home, Nietzsche rejected the idea of God at an early age because—he said—of all the evil in the world. Not long after saying this, Nietzsche died. Someone, wanting to immortalize his famous quote, scribbled inside a bathroom stall:

"God is dead."—Nietzsche

Shortly after that, another person wrote underneath:

"Nietzsche is dead."—God

Ouch! It seems that while people who don't believe in God tend to come and go, God remains. But, honestly, have you ever wondered whether or not God really exists? And if He does exist, how can you be sure? Have you ever wanted to know how to respond to those who deny God's existence? Or maybe you just want to firm up your faith in this area.

This study will present evidence for the existence of God. It isn't designed to prove His existence, but will show how foolish it is to deny God's existence (Psalm 14:1).

1. Imagine a courtroom scene. God is on trial. The prosecuting attorney is an atheist who is trying to disprove the existence of God. Assume his role for a moment. In your presentation, what reasons would you give for not believing there is a God?

2. Now imagine taking your seat as one of the jurors in this case. At this point God takes the stand as His own defense lawyer. The prosecution has presented its case. Now it is God's turn. As He presents the evidence He calls a number of witnesses to the stand. And with this first witness, He asks the members of the jury to—what? Before reading on, briefly jot down reasons God might give for His existence.

REASON 1

REASON 2

REASON 3

REASON 4

2 Witness #1: Listen to Creation

One of the very first evidences for His existence that God might present in court is His creation. In fact, the first thing we learn about God from Scripture is that He is the Creator.

1. When you look around at creation—at the creatures, the oceans, volcanoes, the Tropics, the Arctic (the list could go on)—what does it tell you about God?

2. What does the following Scripture say that creation tells us about God?

Romans 1:20
For since the creation of the world God's invisible qualities—his eternal power and divine nature—have been clearly seen, being understood from what has been made, so that men are without excuse.

3. Why do you think the apostle Paul says that people are without excuse when it comes to not believing in God (Romans 1:20)?

Mind-boggling Tidbits

The Milky Way is 100,000 light years across and contains an estimated 100 billion stars. And it is only one of a billion known galaxies!

The closest galaxy to ours is 200,000 light years away.

If the earth were any closer or farther away from the sun, it would either burn up or freeze.

"Some people say there is a God out there . . . but in my travels around the earth . . . I saw no God or angels. I don't believe in God. I believe in man."—Gherman Titoy, Russian cosmonaut, upon returning from travel in space.

Sir Fred Hoyle, noted British astronomer, has said that the odds of life happening by chance are the odds of a tornado sweeping through a junkyard and assembling a Boeing 747.

Isaiah 45:12
*It is I who made the earth and created mankind upon it. My own hands
stretched out the heavens; I marshaled their starry hosts.*

4. What does God say about Himself in Isaiah 45:12? (See also Job 12:7-9; Psalm 19:1-6; and Malachi 2:10.)

As we look at creation—the universe, the planets and the stars, they all point to a Creator. And with that, God's first witness steps down from the witness stand in the courtroom drama.

3 Witness #2: Listen to Your Conscience

The conscience is our inner part that tells us what is right from wrong. Or, as one little boy put it, "The part of you that makes you tell your mother what you did wrong, before your sister does."

1. According to the following verses, what does Scripture say that people know about God?

Romans 1:19
Since what may be known about God is plain to them,
because God has made it plain to them.

Romans 2:15
Since they show that the requirements of the law are written on their hearts, their consciences also bearing witness, and their thoughts now accusing, now even defending them.

2. According to Romans 1:18, why don't people respond to the conscience that God created them with? Explain your answer in terms that a junior higher would understand.

Creation is God's witness of His existence in the world; conscience is His witness in the heart. One is an external witness; the other is an internal witness.

"But wait," God says, "there is more."

4 Witness #3: Listen to Common Sense

How can common sense and reason tell us there's a God? See if you can come up with an idea or two on your own, before reading on.

EXHIBIT A: THE ARGUMENT FROM CAUSE/EFFECT
1. Every effect has a cause.
2. The universe is an effect.
3. Therefore, the universe has a cause.

Put simply, nothing comes from nothing and something comes from something. Take the World Trade Center. Common sense tells us that something caused it to be (namely, thousands of workmen over several years time!). In the same way, the World Trade Center is an effect which had to have a cause (just as the existence of a watch demands the existence of a watchmaker). Logic demands a cause for humanity and the universe. It is common sense.

EXHIBIT B: THE ARGUMENT FROM DESIGN
1. Every design has a designer.
2. The universe shows design.
3. Therefore, the universe has a designer.

Since a dictionary has both design and order, common sense tells us it was intelligently put together. We don't assume it resulted from an explosion in a print shop! And yet this is what atheists would have us believe about creation—that it just happened without a creator.

The millions of examples of design in our universe and world (the solar system, DNA, the human eye) all point to a designer. Common sense and logic say "yes!"

EXHIBIT C: THE ARGUMENT FROM MORALITY

1. Atheists claim there can't be a God since there is evil and injustice in the world.
2. But if there is no God, where do they get their standard for labeling something as evil or unjust?
3. Therefore, God must exist in order for humanity to make absolute moral judgments about evil and justice.

More Mind-boggling Arguments

Since atheists can't be everywhere at once, they can't possibly say God isn't somewhere they're not. Huh?

Since atheists don't know everything, it is possible that God exists outside their limited knowledge.

It's like trying to convince a person from a primitive culture that cars exist. Since he has never seen a car or ridden in one, his ignorance demands that he deny the existence of them.

In other words, even atheists and many nonreligious people would say it is wrong to needlessly kill someone else. Most of them oppose child abuse, rape, robbery, and other heinous crimes. But why? Who says those things are absolutely wrong?

To be honest, they must agree that in order to label something as right or wrong, there must be a final authority or source of morality to appeal to. Otherwise, it's just one person's opinion against another's. So, someone must have caused us to be, because people believe in right and wrong.

5 Witness #4: Listen to the Credibility of Scripture

The fourth witness to testify for the defense is God's Word. While the Bible wasn't written to prove the existence of God, it affirms it over and over again.

The Bible begins with the words, "In the beginning God . . . " (Genesis 1:1). Throughout its pages, the Bible declares or assumes the existence of the Creator.

1. What does Scripture claim about itself in II Timothy 3:16 and II Peter 1:21?

But how do we know the Bible is trustworthy?

EXHIBIT D: PROPHECY SAYS SO

Isaiah 7:14 accurately predicted the virgin birth of Jesus Christ. His race, tribe, betrayal, trial, death, burial, and resurrection are also perfectly prophesied. More than sixty prophecies were accurately foretold thousands of years before they took place!

EXHIBIT E: HISTORY SAYS SO

The Hittites mentioned in Joshua 1:4 are mentioned more than ten times in the Old Testament. But for years archaeologists and scholars denied the existence of such a people. They used this information to try to discredit the Bible until 1906 when archaeologists digging in Turkey found—you guessed it—evidence of the Hittites! So far, archaeological discoveries have contributed a lot of evidence to reinforce the reliability of the Bible.

EXHIBIT F: SCIENCE SAYS SO

The Bible is not a science book, yet it is amazingly accurate as an ancient book. Scripture speaks specifically about the sciences of:

- geology (Isaiah 40:12; Job 26:7)

- physiology (Leviticus 17:11) [It took until 1615 for William Harvey to "discover" the circulation of the blood, yet God's Word mentioned it thousands of years before!]

- astronomy (Jeremiah 33:22—Ptolemy [the Alexandrian astronomer] said there were 1,056 stars in the sky while Kepler claimed there were 1,055. Finally Galileo correctly agreed with Scripture in saying there were too many to count.)

- hydrology (Ecclesiastes 1:7—evaporation, condensation, precipitation).

6 Witness #5: Listen to Christ

God's last word concerning evidence of His existence was Jesus Christ.

1. What does John 1:14 say about humanity's knowledge of the existence of God?

2. List at least four verses in which Jesus—indirectly or directly—says God exists.

3. What does Jesus' life, death, and resurrection say to you about the existence of God?

What about the millions of people throughout history whose lives have been radically changed by God? Could someone who doesn't exist change murderers, satanists, thieves, rapists, convicts, emperors, kings, Nazis, scientists, lawyers, doctors, athletes, actors, billionaires, and high school students into committed disciples of Jesus Christ?

4. Do you still have questions about the existence of God? If so, write them down here and begin to seek out answers for them.

5. To find out what atheism ultimately leads to, read Romans 1:21-32. Then draw a symbol that represents the sin and confusion described there.

So why get all bent out of shape trying to figure out if God exists or not? Because three logical and crucial questions concerning Him demand answers.

    a. If there is a God, what is He like?

    b. Can He be known? and

    c. Am I accountable to Him?

6. Acts 17:30, 31 gives another regarding the belief of God's existence. What is is it?

7. What about Christians? What did God tell Jeremiah to make his ultimate goal in life (Jeremiah 9:23, 24)?

8. What effect do you think this ultimate goal should have on your life? How should it change it?

KEEP In Mind

Many years ago, a young missionary from the United States wanted to tell an unreached tribe from deep in the rain forests of South America about God. The young man worked many long, discouraging months trying to figure out its complicated language. When he finally felt confident enough, he translated John 3:16, went to the tribal prince, and said, "For God so loved the world that he gave his one and only Son, that whoever believes in him shall not perish but have eternal life."

Before he could find out if he was understood, the prince took off running through the village, screaming wildly. The missionary followed him as he ran from village to village, hut to hut screaming at the top of his lungs. When he finally stopped, the missionary began to apologize, asking what he had done to offend.

But the tribal prince replied, "No, no, you don't understand. My people have known for centuries that there was a God. But we never knew He had done anything to help us know Him! I have been running to every village, screaming that good news to my people!"

God exists.

He can be known.

You can know Him!

By the way, the jury found God innocent of "not existing."

PRAY About It

Take a minute in prayer to thank God that He is real, alive, near, and knowable. Ask Him to help you know Him more personally as you study His Word in the upcoming weeks. Write out your prayer here.

This page is for your prayers. Write them out.

Write prayers of praise. Give adoration to God simply for who He is and what He is like. Then write about what's going on in your life right now. Praise and thank God for hearing your requests and answering your prayers. As you talk to God about your life and your relationship with Him, keep track of how He's answering your prayers and what He's doing in your life.

WEEK 2 Awesome God!

The Power of God

1 Superpower

It can't be that bad.
I don't have time to worry about it. I've got work to do.
I want to videotape it and send it to network news.

When Hurricane Hugo finally arrived in September 1989, most of the residents (the wise ones) of historic Charleston, South Carolina ran for their lives as it slammed into the coastline, packing 140 mile-per-hour winds and a 17-foot-high wall of water. Hugo ripped roofs off buildings, uprooted huge trees, blew yachts into the streets, and leveled homes to the ground. It continued up the eastern coastline on a reign of destruction and terror until it finally died down.

When all was said and done, 28 people died, 90,000 were left homeless, and damage was estimated in the billions. Seashells were found as far as 200 miles inland.

That's power—mega-power.

What kinds of power have you ever personally seen? Check off the ones that apply.

- ☐ **A raging river at flood stage**   ☐ **Thunder and lightning**
- ☐ **Tornado**   ☐ **Fire**   ☐ **Earthquake**
- ☐ **Hurricane**   ☐ **Jet taking off at an airport**
- ☐ **Avalanche**   ☐ **Bomb explosion**
- ☐ **Tidal wave**   ☐ **Monster trucks race**
- ☐ **President or Vice President of the U.S.**   ☐ **Indy 500**
- ☐ **God's power**
- ☐ **Other:** _____

If you checked off that you have seen God's power, what do you mean by that? Explain. If you didn't check it off, explain why you think you have not witnessed God's power.

During this study, you will discover the answers to three basic questions concerning the power of God:

1. What does it mean?

2. What does it look like?

3. How do I experience it?

2 The Story Behind God's Power

1. Would you be hard pressed to explain God's power to someone else? How does God's Word describe His own power?

- Isaiah 1:24

- Genesis 18:14

- Job 42:1, 2

2. From these verses, write out your own definition of the power of God.

God's power is:

3. List a few examples of God's power as described in the Bible (without looking them up).

God's power is His ability to do what He chooses. Theologians call this omnipotence (*omni* means all; *potent* means power). God is all-powerful, or better, infinitely powerful.

4. Look up the following examples of God's power and give each one a movie title—real or made up. The comments following each passage may spark some ideas for titles.

- Genesis 19:23-25

Can you imagine witnessing this event? These wicked cities were so wrapped up in their sin, they didn't have a clue God would actually judge them. But God ignited something like a nuclear explosion that incinerated every living thing in and around the cities. If you use your imagination, you might have seen a blast of glowing chemicals consuming everything in its path—which apparently was lagging too far behind the fleeing Lot (Genesis 19:26).

- Hebrews 11:29

A teacher once told her second-grade class that this event didn't really happen as the Bible records it. "It wasn't a real sea Israel crossed. It was only four inches deep." To which little Johnny blurted out, "Wow! That's an even greater miracle. The whole Egyptian army drowned in four inches of water!"

But seriously, several million Jews walked across a major body of water on dry ground! And it took them quite awhile. Shall we say God merely "sneezed" and those massive walls of water were held back (Exodus 15:8)? Then the water returned to it's normal state just in time to drown Pharaoh's entire army (Exodus 14:26-28). And do you know what Israel did in response to this display of God's power? They feared God and put their trust in Him (vs. 31) and sang a song about the event (Exodus 15).

- Joshua 10:12, 13

Some scholars think God slowed the earth's rotation enough to prolong daylight for Joshua and his army to win the battle against the Amorites. Who knows. Others believe He supernaturally extended the day by refracting the light of the sun. Either way, it was pretty powerful.

5. If you could personally witness any Bible event in which God displayed His power, which one would it be and why?

6. What do these events tell you about God's power?

7. You read about the Israelites' reaction to one of God's displays of power (Exodus 14, 15). How do you think you would respond to such awesome examples of God's power?

8. Have you ever wondered why God doesn't seem to part seas and lengthen days in this age as He did in Bible times? Why do you think this is so?

9. Do you think today's catastrophes are displays of God's power or not? Explain.

3 The Powerful and the Powerless

Perhaps you have wondered whether an all-powerful God could really care about little ol' you. Even though you may seem small in comparison to God's mightiness, you and your needs are not unimportant or insignificant to Him.

The truth is that God has already displayed His power in you. To find out how, check out these verses. Write key words that identify God's power at work in your life.

- Romans 1:16

- I Corinthians 10:13

- John 10:28, 29

- Isaiah 40:28-31

- Ephesians 3:20, 21

God uses His power to create earthshaking events, but He also uses it to meet our needs. The same power that spoke the world into existence and raised Christ from the dead is available to us at home, school, work, and with friends. God is ready and willing to use His power for you when you ask for it. He can change things and He can help us cope with life as we find it.

KEEP In Mind

These principles can enable you to experience God's power in your life:

1. *Put yourself in a position to experience His power. You could:*

- Set a goal to tell a certain number of people about Christ this year.

- Ask God to help you raise funds for a missionary, your own missions trip, or for college.

- Run for student government.

- Ask God to provide a job for you.

- Start a Christian club on your campus, or be involved in the leadership and planning.

- Go on a missions trip this summer.

- Ask God for the ability and desire to obey your parents and to maintain a good attitude toward the relationship.

Remember, Moses would never have seen the parting of the Red Sea unless he had stepped out in faith to lead God's people from Egypt. Joshua would have never seen the sun stand still unless he had been obedient to go to battle for God. Elijah would have never seen God show His awesome power if he had not decided to take on the 400 prophets of Baal (I Kings 18). So attempt something great for God!

2. *Realize you can never achieve your goals in your own strength.* When you feel weak as you work toward your goals, rely on God's strength (II Corinthians 12:9). Have the same attitude Paul had when he wrote "I can do everything through him who gives me strength" (Philippians 4:13). That trust includes the lows as well as the highs of life (Philippians 4:12).

PRAY About It

When the Lord revealed Himself to Abraham in Genesis 17:1, He used the Hebrew words *El-Shaddai* to describe Himself. *El-Shaddai* is Hebrew for "God Almighty." This name for God is found 31 times in the book of Job and 17 times elsewhere in the Scriptures. Meditate on His name for a few minutes before beginning your prayer time. Then talk with God about the areas in life in which you need His power. Jot down key words for a few of these areas of need.

Continue your list of prayer requests and answers that you started last week.

WEEK 3 Who's in Control?

The Sovereignty of God

1 Ride 'em Cowboy!

Have you ever felt "out of control"? I have (that's me, Jeff, the author of this book).

It happened on my honeymoon at a resort in the Allegheny mountains of western Virginia. My wife, who had taken twelve years of riding lessons wanted me to go horseback riding with her. I agreed, although I wasn't thrilled about the fact that a guide had to accompany us—after all, we were, well, honeymooners.

Anyway, I knew how to ride. You see, I was raised on *Bonanza* and *Gunsmoke*, and John Wayne was my hero. But once we arrived at the stable, I was surprised to see English, not Western, saddles. Now everyone knows that Western saddles are macho and English saddles are for sissies. Even worse was that I had to wear one of those silly-looking riding helmets (I know, I know, better safe than sorry).

After a short, slow ride, the guide asked if we wanted to run the horses. Before I could scream "No way!!!" my precious bride yelled "Sure!!!" And off we went.

For the next fifty minutes, I danced at death's doorstep. I immediately let go of the reigns and reached for the "horn." But there is no horn on an English saddle. So I shoved my hands underneath the saddle and held on for life. We galloped along trails with steep drop-offs. One misstep, and I was a goner. Even worse was the fact that my helmet, which was too big, had fallen down over my face and was blocking my vision. I was too terrified to let go of the saddle to fix it. My head kept hitting tree branches as we raced through the forest. I was officially out of control. No one could hear my screams because the helmet muffled my voice. I frantically felt for emergency brakes, airbags, parachutes, whatever.

After fifty minutes on the horse from Hades, it stopped. I pried my hands from underneath the saddle to find every knuckle bloodied. The hair on the inside of my legs had been "teased" from all the rubbing. My head was throbbing and my back was in pain. But at least it was over (or so I thought). My horse then proceeded to trip over a rock and take off on another gallop. HELP!

Now that is a bad day!

Ever had one of those days when you felt as if you were in a tailspin? Perhaps nothing is going right for you. You oversleep the day of a big exam. Your car gets a flat tire on the way to work. Your mom gets bad news from the doctor. Your first choice for college turns you down. Even worse, you look around and see a world that seems to be out of control as well. Governments change hands overnight. Injustice and evil abound. Wars go on. Innocent people suffer while guilty ones go free. Violence, crime, disease, famine, and rampant drug abuse all seem to suggest that ours is a culture of chaos. A recent poll found that 65 percent of Americans believe the world is out of control.

Does God know what is going on and does He care? How do you make sense out of all of this?

The answer lies in the sovereignty of God.

1. To find out what this means, read the following passages and write down what they tell you about God's sovereignty.

- Psalms 115:3; 135:6; Daniel 4:35

2. People today talk a lot about rights and freedoms. According to the previous verses, what rights does God have?

2 "Reign" in the Forecast

Have you heard the story about the man who booked a flight on the world's first fully automated airline? Everything would be run by computers, he was told—no pilot, no copilot, no navigator—fully automated and faultless. Though he had doubts, he began to relax as the jet taxied down the runway and took off. Then a voice on the intercom (fully automated, of course) said, "Ladies and gentlemen, welcome to Microchip Airways, the world's first fully automated computer airline. Please sit back and relax in the security of knowing that nothing can go wrong . . . go wrong . . . go wrong . . . . "

Oh, stewardess!

Many people label God as they would label Microchip Airways—having good intentions, impressive, but simply unable to control everything. It's like the church that misprinted the pastor's sermon title as "Our God Resigns," instead of "Our God Reigns." Some people seem to think God has resigned from ruling His universe.

1. But what does the Bible say about God's rule and His ability to control His universe?

- Psalm 45:6

- Isaiah 40:21-24

2. What did God's sovereignty and control mean to Israel? Read Psalm 46:1-3 and complete the following sentences:

Psalm 46:1-3
God is our refuge and strength, an ever-present help in trouble. Therefore we will not fear, though the earth give way and the mountains fall into the heart of the sea, though its waters roar and foam and the mountains quake with their surging.

God is our:

Therefore we will not:

Even if:

God is still in control.

3. How would you fill in the same sentences?

God is my:

Therefore I will not:

Even if:

God is still in control.

Maybe you still wonder *If God is in control, then why is the world so messed up?* Think of God's sovereignty like being on a cruise ship. While on board, you have the freedom to do many things—eat, swim, jog, play basketball, go to shows, work out, walk—yet all the while, the captain is at the wheel guiding the ship and everyone on board toward their destination. In the same way, God can accomplish all His purposes without controlling every person's actions. Though people have freedom, God is still at the wheel and in control of the ship!

4. Think of another similar analogy for this idea. Be prepared to explain how your analogy relates to the cruise ship example.

3 What, Me Worry?

God is King. He does what He pleases. He rules over all. So what difference does it make to you? Let's answer that question by examining what impact God's sovereignty has had on the lives of other people.

1. JOSEPH

See Genesis 37; 39:6-23; 40:23.

What happened to Joseph that may have caused him to question God's sovereignty?

According to Genesis 50:20, what perspective did Joseph gain concerning God's sovereignty in his life?

2. JESUS

See Acts 2:22, 23.

What does verse 23 say about God's sovereignty in the death of Christ?

In what way did God plan this tragedy for good?

3. YOU

See Romans 8:28.

What phrase does Paul use to describe the confidence we should have in God? Circle one:

And we think . . .   And we know . . .

And we hope . . .   And we are pretty sure . . .

And we suppose . . .   And we sort of believe . . .

Describe an event in your life that you now view as consistent with the truth expressed in Romans 8:28. What did this event teach you about God's sovereignty?

Are there any events in your life that have caused or are causing you to question the validity of Romans 8:28? For example, you may have suffered through a family breakup, or had destructive habits, or been mistreated and abused as a child. Or maybe you've had a hard life in general. These kinds of things are the "all things" God uses. Could God be so big, so in control that He could create something good from difficult circumstances?

What personal circumstance do you need God to work "for the good of those who love Him and are called according to His purpose" right now?

People may think they are in control, but the Bible says God is working behind the scenes, bringing history along to conform to His plan. Even so, there have been some earthly rulers who thought they could run the world better than God. They challenged God's sovereignty—and regretted it. Maybe you've heard of the following cocky criminals.

• PHARAOH—alias "Pharaoh the Proud" (Exodus 4–12). The Egyptian ruler (Moses' adversary) who arrogantly challenged God's authority. God gave Pharaoh ten "object lessons" (better known as the ten plagues) to convince him of His authority. God sovereignly raised up Pharaoh to show His great power (Romans 9:17).

• KING AHAB—alias "Ahab the Arrogant" (I Kings 16–22). God told Ahab not to go into battle against the Arameans. But he challenged God's sovereignty by going anyway. Ahab disguised himself as an ordinary soldier, but a stray arrow pierced through an opening in his armor, and the dogs licked up his blood just as God's prophet had predicted.

• KING NEBUCHADNEZZAR—alias "Never Be Lesser Nebuchadnezzar" (Daniel 4:30-37). As King of Babylon, he praised and exalted himself. God gave Him a ride he never forgot. You must read this one!

• KING HEROD—alias "Herod the Haughty" (Acts 12:21-23). Herod set himself up to be worshiped as a god. But the Lord struck him with worms and he died. God shares His sovereignty with no one.

These men thought they could outrank the God of heaven. Big mistake! They opposed His sovereign right to rule and to control the affairs of men. But God always proves He is in control. He can even change the hearts of rulers to do what He wants them to (Proverbs 21:1).

PRAY About It

A painting entitled "Peace" depicts a fierce storm that is causing waves to violently crash against jagged rocks. It seems anything but peaceful. But down in a small corner of the painting, tucked away in the rocks, is a little bird sleeping on her nest totally oblivious to the raging storm around her. That is peace.

One of the secrets to having peace is to trust that God is in control. Write a prayer asking for that kind of peace or for God to sustain your trust in Him. The prayer is started here for you. You can write specifically about the personal circumstance you may have described in the last question in Section III.

Don't forget to continue tracking all of your requests and answers, too.

Lord of All,

WEEK 4 ◄ Holy Smokes!

The Holiness of God

1 But He's Bigger and Better Than Me

I was 155 pounds of pure determination as I stepped onto the basketball court to play center. It was the regional high school basketball tournament. The stands were packed with parents and local fans who came to see the up-and-coming high school hoopsters. On court I reached out to shake my opponent's hand and found that it wrapped twice around mine. I found myself staring into the numbers on his chest! Things weren't looking good at this point. I began to feel sick.

This 6' 9" center (I'm 5' 10") out jumped me all night. When the mercy killing was over (they whipped us good), I congratulated this fellow (by this time I was calling him sir). He introduced himself and I vowed to remember his name. But I didn't have to try very hard, because his name appeared in the sports pages for the next several years. He was the most outstanding high school basketball player in North Carolina his senior year, and he won a national championship at the University of North Carolina. He then became an NBA All-Star with the Los Angeles Lakers. His name is James Worthy.

When I think back on my memorable experience with James, one word comes to mind—I-N-T-I-M-I-D-A-T-I-O-N. He was bigger, stronger, and taller than I was. He could jump higher and rebound better. He was intimidating. I was intimidated.

When I reflect on the nature of God, one aspect of His character intimidates me more than the others. It towers above all of us, dwarfing us. There can even be a sense of dread as we approach it. It is God's holiness.

Perhaps no other aspect of God's character is ignored as much as this one. God's holiness is misunderstood, misrepresented, and misapplied. But when properly understood, it can transform one's life.

1. Here is something to help you feel a little intimidated. Rate God's holiness (G); then rate your own (U) by placing the appropriate letter somewhere along the following scale. 1 = completely evil; 5 = perfectly holy

1	2	3	4	5

2. Put a check mark next to the activities that you think are holy. In the last spot, fill in an activity that *you* think is holy.

❑ Feeding a stray cat.

❑ Reading the Bible.

❑ Not repeating a rumor about someone.

❑ Listening to Christian music.

❑ Obeying a stop sign.

❑ Telling someone about Christ.

❑ Praying for someone else.

❑ Going on a short-term missions trip.

❑ Other: _____

3. Holy X-ray! Before you get into a serious study of holiness, enjoy the lighter side of the subject. How many of these words and phrases containing the word holy can you define? Most of the answers are in the dictionary—but don't look until you're finished.

holy city

holy of holies

holy oil

holy order

holystone

holy underwear

holy war

holy water

holy writ

Holy Grail

Holy Joe

Holy Mackerel

Holy Roller

Holy Roman Empire

Holy Saturday

Holy See

Holy Smokes, Batman!

Holy Thursday

Holy Week

Holy Year

2 Holiness Too Hot to Touch

Even though you just filled in the holiness rating, do you really know what it means to say that God is holy or that a person is holy? Let's check out God's holiness first.

Isaiah 57:15
For this is what the high and lofty One says—he who lives forever, whose name is holy: "I live in a high and holy place, but also with him who is contrite and lowly in spirit, to revive the spirit of the lowly and to revive the heart of the contrite."

1. What do you think it means when Scripture says that God is "high and lofty"?

2. What two things are described as holy?

3. What contrast is stated here and how do you think holiness relates to both extremes?

Now read Isaiah 6:1-7.

4. How does Isaiah describe God's holiness?

5. How does Isaiah describe himself in relation to God's holiness? And where would you put an "I" for Isaiah along the holiness scale in Section I?

6. How is Isaiah made acceptable in God's presence and what does it have in common with the way that you have been made acceptable to God?

7. Read the following passages. If this was all you knew about God, what would you think of Him?

Numbers 23:19
God is not a man, that he should lie, nor a son of man, that he should change his mind. Does he speak and then not act? Does he promise and not fulfill?

Isaiah 55:8, 9
"For my thoughts are not your thoughts, neither are your ways my ways," declares the Lord. "As the heavens are higher than the earth, so are my ways higher than your ways and my thoughts than your thoughts."

3 Blindfolded Angels

As Isaiah's vision continues, he sees another facet of God's holiness. Read Isaiah 6:2.

1. Why do you think that the seraphim covered their faces and feet in God's presence (Exodus 3:4-6 and 19:20, 21)?

2. How does John describe God's holiness in I John 1:5?

So think of God's holiness as His absolute, 100 percent, perfect moral purity. He was, is, and always will be free from sin.

4 What, Me Holy?

1. You have read how Isaiah felt in the holy presence of God. Now take a look at the following passages and describe in one or two words (or a symbol) how each of these people reacted to God's holy presence.

David—Psalm 139:23

John—Revelation 1:17

Moses—Exodus 3:6

Daniel—Daniel 10:4-9

The men with Daniel—Daniel 10:7

Ezekiel—Ezekiel 3:23

2. If you had been these guys, how do you think you would have reacted?

3. Do you remember how you reacted the first time you realized the truth about God—that He is Lord and Savior—or the first time you became aware of His presence? Describe it.

4. In a sense, you are in the presence of God all the time since His Holy Spirit lives in all believers. Has knowing this truth changed the way you live and act? Identify some of the main areas of your life in which you act as if you don't realize that God is present (for example, your thoughts, speech, dating relationships, etc.).

5. Understanding God's holiness can also motivate you to worship Him with renewed enthusiasm and with a pure heart. In what ways do you think your worship time needs to change?

6. How can you practically and realistically obey the command in I Peter 1:14-16? Be specific.

KEEP In Mind

The point is that we can never know who we really are until we see who God really is. His holiness is the giant searchlight shining into every corner of our lives. It reveals all our hidden secrets and our every sin. That thought can be intimidating but it can also motivate us to ask God to clean up our lives! And understanding God's holiness can encourage us to worship Him in a new light with new enthusiasm.

PRAY About It

Complete this prayer.

Lord, Your holiness . . .

Lord, my holiness . . .

Don't forget to keep track of continuing prayer requests and answers.

WEEK 5 Safe At Home

The Love of God

1 No Cuddling Allowed

In the thirteenth century, King Frederick II attempted an interesting experiment. He attempted to raise a group of children without any maternal affection. His goal was to see what language the children would speak if no one spoke to them beforehand. So he brought in foster mothers and nurses to bathe and feed the children, but they were not allowed to play with them, speak to them, or cuddle them. The king wanted to see if the little ones might begin to speak Hebrew, the oldest language, or Greek, or Latin, or Arabic, or even the language of their natural parents. But King Frederick's labor was in vain, for all the children soon died. They simply could not survive without the loving words and care of another human being.

What happened to those poor children is labeled "failure to thrive" by physicians today. This is a scientific way of saying "people can't live without love." Psychologists agree that everyone has two basic needs—to feel loved and to feel significant. You probably know people who go to great lengths to meet these two needs in their lives. Some look for love in relationships. Others search for significance in popularity, success, or achievement. Unfortunately, our world tends to offer broken promises, broken homes, and broken relationships. People young and old feel unloved, unwanted, and unnecessary.

Yet most people don't understand that the Creator of the universe has declared a perfect love for them that can transform them and meet all of their needs. But what exactly does it mean to say, "God loves us?" What is His love like? How can we understand it and experience it? How can we know it's for real? These are some of the questions you will explore in the next few pages.

1. To recognize how important love is in your own life, quickly list the names of family, friends, and relatives who love you and whom you love. You may be surprised to find that you need a lot more space for names than is allotted here.

2 Just An Old Testament Love Song

Sometimes we think of God as being judgmental in the Old Testament and loving in the New Testament. After all, in the O.T., you tend to focus on the fire and brimstone, the worldwide flood, earthquakes, fire from heaven, poisonous snakes, ten plagues, disease, famine—in other words, judgment. In the N.T., you tend to focus on Jesus going around healing and forgiving people. Yet it is safe to say that both judgment and love are thoroughly a part of both Testaments. Woven into incredible Old Testament events is the love of God for His people, the nation of Israel. And now that you belong to the Lord, you can experience that same love in your life!

1. What is the first thing that comes to your mind when you think of God in the Old Testament?

2. What have you thought about God's toughness/tenderness at different stages of your life? Circle the appropriate number on each scale:

As a child, I thought God was:

1	2	3	4	5
Ruthless	Tough	Mix of tender & tough	Tender	Purely loving

As an adolescent, I thought God was:

1	2	3	4	5
Ruthless	Tough	Mix of tender & tough	Tender	Purely loving

Now, I think God is:

1	2	3	4	5
Ruthless	Tough	Mix of tender & tough	Tender	Purely loving

3. When God chose Israel (and you), what was His motivation (Deuteronomy 7:7, 8)?

Deuteronomy 7:7, 8
The Lord did not set his affection on you and choose you because you were more numerous than other peoples, for you were the fewest of all peoples. But it was because the Lord loved you and kept the oath he swore to your forefathers that he brought you out with a mighty hand and redeemed you from the land of slavery, from the power of Pharaoh king of Egypt.

4. Circle the words and phrases in Deuteronomy 7:7, 8 that indicate God's love.

5. What kind of love does God have for you? See what you can discover from the following Scriptures. Complete the sentences using your own words.

- Psalm 103:11

God's love for me is . . .

- Jeremiah 31:3

God's love for me is . . .

- Psalm 117:2

God's love for me is . . .

- Psalm 63:3

God's love for me is . . .

6. When do you most doubt God's love for you?

7. Do any of the previous verses address your doubts? If so, how?

8. Contrast the love of God with the love you find in the world. Base your ideas on the verses you've read so far and any other verses that you are familiar with that speak of God's love.

God's Love   World's Love

A.

B.

C.

The whole concept of love that is faithful or committed has lost much of it's meaning today. Instead there is plenty of conditional love to go around, which says:

- I love you if . . .
- I love you when . . .
- I love you because . . .

9. Has anyone's love ever disappointed you? In what way?

God's love is not conditional (nor is it deserved). You did nothing to qualify for it. It is available to you no matter what kind of sinner you are. God's love is faithful even when you aren't. His love for you is loyal even when your love for Him isn't. No wonder David said God's love is better than life! That's love—Old Testament style. Not bad at all!

3 Love Me Tender

Here are three powerful images God chose to explain how much He loves you.

Image #1—God's love is like a _____ love (Isaiah 63:16).

How does Scripture further define this kind of love? Use words or simple drawings to answer.

- Psalm 103:13

- Romans 8:15

- Proverbs 3:12

Psalm 68:5 also tells us God is the "father to the fatherless." He is the perfect parent! And get this—He even lets you call Him "Daddy" (as Galatians 4:6 indicates). He's never too tired to listen and He always has time for you. And He is good at showing you how much He loves you (Romans 5:8; Lamentations 3:22, 23).

Image #2—God's love is like a _____ love (Psalm 23:1).

How does Scripture further define this kind of love? Use words or simple drawings to answer.

- Psalm 23:1, 2

- Ezekiel 34:11, 12

- John 10:11

- Titus 3:4-6

God's love is like a tower (Proverbs 18:10). It protects us like a shepherd protects his sheep. It watches over us, cares for us and, like a good shepherd, searches for us when we lose our way. That's not a bad deal!

Image #3—God's love is like a _____ love (Isaiah 54:5).

How does Scripture further define this kind of love? Use words or simple drawings to answer.

- Ephesians 5:25-29

- Isaiah 62:5

- II Corinthians 11:2

This may sound a little strange if you're unmarried, especially if you're a guy! But the Bible says, as believers, we are the "bride" of Christ (Revelation 19:7).

4 All You Need Is (His) Love

When you think about it, the main thing you really need in life is for God to love you. If everything else falls apart and if everyone else fails you, God's love for you is still there. So how should you respond to this offer of love? Here are four ways:

1. Accept It

- Because His love is lavished on us (I John 3:1).
- Because His love can be personally experienced (Ephesians 3:19; Galatians 2:20).
- Because God loves you like He loves _____ (John 17:23).

2. Enjoy It

- Because there's plenty of it (Psalm 86:15).
- Because nothing can _____ you from it (Romans 8:35-39)!

3. Hope In It

- Because it will get you through tough times (Isaiah 43:1-7).
- Because His love takes away your _____ (I John 4:18-21).

4. Share It

- Because He has loved you first (I John 4:19).
- Because this demonstrates that you belong to Him (I John 4:7-19).

Once, after lecturing on a famous university campus, theologian Karl Barth, was asked, "Dr. Barth, what is the deepest theological thought that has ever crossed your mind?" The aged theologian stroked his chin, thought for a moment, and then replied, "The deepest thought that has ever crossed my mind is this: Jesus loves me, this I know, for the Bible tells me so."

It almost sounds too simple, doesn't it? But it is true.

We all need love, and God has showered His children with a love that never lets go. He loves you when you don't love Him back, whether or not you feel loved, and even when you don't understand His love. It is an unconditional, uncommon, unchanging, and unfailing love. It depends on Him, not you. It makes you feel safe, secure, and special. It removes your fears. Isn't it great to be loved like that?

PRAY About It

Write out a prayer in which you thank the Lord for specific ways in which His love has made a difference in your life. Don't forget to keep track of continuing prayer requests and answers.

God the Son

Jesus Christ.

Fully God, yet fully human.

It boggles the mind, this phenomenon of God's master plan—sending His own Son to become human flesh to bear our burden of sin.

You'll be looking at the events surrounding and concerning Jesus' birth, His life, His death, His resurrection, and His claim to be God.

But trying to figure out and explain the phenomenon of God the Son isn't the real issue. The real issue is believing in Jesus, and what His life and death means to a world of sinners who deserve condemnation.

This unit will help both solidify that belief in your own life, as well as enable you to better explain God the Son to others—so that they might believe as well.

WEEK ⟨6⟩ Baby Grand!

The Coming of Jesus

1 A Legend for All Times

He was born in A.D. 280 in a small Asian town. His wealthy parents died while he was young but not before they had instilled in him the gift of faith. When little Nicholas grew up, he lived a life of sacrifice and love. In fact, he became so respected that when his town needed a bishop, he was selected.

Nicholas was imprisoned for his faith by the Emperor Diocletian, but was later released by the Emperor Constantine. He spent the rest of his short life begging food for the poor, and giving away money to little girls so they would have a dowry to get a husband. The story most often repeated is about how he would disguise himself and go out to give gifts to poor children. He ended up giving away everything he had, and in the year 314, at the age of 34, he died.

Today, there are more church buildings named after Saint Nicholas than any other person in history. Unfortunately, his true image has changed through time. The poet Clement Moore gave him a red nose and eight tiny reindeer. And Thomas Nast, the illustrator, made him fat and old and gave him a red suit trimmed in fur. Others have changed his name—Belsnickle, Kris Kringle, and of course, Santa Claus. But what's important about Nicholas is that he illustrated something of the mind of Christ, and through his unselfish love, he touched his world. If he were alive today, he no doubt would be surprised at the way his image (among other things) has pushed aside Christ as the focus of Christmas.

At the first Christmas, some 2,000 years ago, the God of the universe came to visit our planet. The Incarnation means God became human; He became one of us. Take a closer look at this mystery.

2 Mary Had a Little Lamb

The first coming of Christ is packed with miraculous events. Angel choirs appearing to shepherds, supernatural lights in the sky, God speaking through dream visions, and personal visits by the archangel Gabriel. But no miracle was as incredible as the virgin birth of Jesus through a girl named Mary. Just how did this happen? Why was the virgin birth necessary? And why is it so important to your faith today?

1. List every fact you learn about Mary in Luke 1:26, 27. (By the way, Bible scholars believe Mary was between thirteen and sixteen years old at this time!)

2. Summarize Gabriel's message to her in one sentence (Luke 1:28-33). Or, if you are feeling rather creative, state it in the form of a limerick. (There once was . . .)

3. How did she respond to this announcement (vss. 34, 38)?

If Jesus was fully unique (being God as well as human), we would expect His entrance to planet Earth to be absolutely unique. Jesus was the only human being in history to be conceived without the agency of a human father (Matthew 1:18, 20; Luke 1:34, 35). Technically, this should be called Christ's virgin conception. Christians commonly call it the virgin birth.

3 Amazing Predictions!

Down through the years, babies have been born in unusual and unique ways. They have been delivered on hospital lawns, in the back seats of taxicabs, and even on airplanes. Even so, Jesus' birth was unlike any other because He was born of a virgin. No one had done that before and no one has done it since.

But there is another reason why Christ's birth is so unique. His birth was actually foretold hundreds of years before it happened. Modern medicine enables doctors to determine the approximate arrival time of a baby once it is conceived. But try predicting a birth and the events surrounding it 700 years before it happens . . . and with amazing accuracy!

What exactly was predicted in the *Old* Testament about the birth of Christ?

- He will be born of a virgin (Isaiah 7:14).

- He will be called _____ (Isaiah 7:14).

- The place of His birth will be _____ (Micah 5:2).

- He would be born of the seed of _____ (Genesis 3:15).

- He would be born of the seed of _____ (Genesis 22:18).

- He would come from the tribe of _____ (Genesis 49:10).

- He would come from the family of _____ (Isaiah 11:1).

- He would come from the house of _____ (Jeremiah 23:5).

1. Match these predictions with their fulfillments in the New Testament by putting the appropriate letter from the second column into the correct blank in the first column.

1.____ Born of a virgin

2.____ The seed of woman

3.____ Born in Bethlehem

4.____ The seed of Abraham

5.____ The tribe of Judah

6.____ The house of David

7.____ The family of Jesse

a. Galatians 4:4

b. Galatians 3:16

c. Matthew 1:18, 24, 25

d. Luke 3:23, 32

e. Luke 3:23, 31; Revelation 22:16

f. Hebrews 7:14

g. Matthew 2:1

Granted, some people can control some things about their lives, but they can't choose their mother, their hometown, their race . . . unless they are God!

In the book *Science Speaks*, Dr. Peter W. Stoner calculates the odds of a person fulfilling just 48 of the 300 messianic prophecies found in the Bible. Stoner mathematically concludes those odds to be 1 in 10^{157}! To illustrate those odds, he uses the example of the electron. If you were to count 250 electrons per minute, you would spend 190 million years counting them. (By the way, they would all fit in one inch. Is your brain overheating yet?)

Dr. Stoner then says that if you selected one electron from among the trillions that you just counted, marked it, stirred it back in with the unmarked ones, and allowed a blindfolded man one attempt at finding the marked electron, his chance of finding it would be this: the same chance as one man fulfilling just 48 of the 300 prophecies about the Messiah!

JESUS FULFILLED ALL 300 PROPHECIES PERFECTLY.

4 God in a Bod

A Persian monarch named Shah Abbis loved his people very much. To know and understand them better, he dressed in various disguises and mingled with his subjects.

One day, disguised as a poor man, Shah Abbis left the palace and went to the public baths. There, in a tiny cellar sat a man who tended the furnace. At mealtime the monarch shared a small meal with the man and talked with him. Again and again he visited, and the man grew to love him.

Eventually, the Shah revealed his true identity, expecting the poor man to ask for some gift from him. But the man just sat gazing at his ruler with wonder. At last he spoke. "You left your palace and your glory to sit with me in this dark place," said the man, "to eat the food I eat, to care whether my heart is glad or sorry. On others you may bestow rich presents, but to me you have given yourself, and my only wish is that you never withdraw the gift of your friendship."

Perhaps the greatest mystery in all the Bible is how God became a human and lived with His creation. He ate our food, wore our clothes, and felt what we feel. You've examined His miraculous birth and the amazing prophecies surrounding His entrance into the world. Now it is time to look closely at Jesus—the Son of God, the Son of Man.

1. How do John 1:1 and Philippians 2:8 appear to contradict each other?

2. What do these verses show you about Jesus' humanness?
   - Matthew 4:1
   - Matthew 4:2
   - John 4:6
   - John 19:28

3. What do these verses show you about Jesus' deity?

- Mark 4:39, 41

(More about the deity of Christ in Week 10 of this book.)

There is a sense in which it is difficult to completely comprehend that Jesus could be both fully God and fully human at the same time. But that is precisely why He is so unique in history.

4. Why did Jesus come to us? See what you can discover from these verses:

- John 1:18

Jesus came to . . .

- I John 3:8

Jesus came to . . .

- Hebrews 4:15; 5:1, 2

Jesus came to . . .

- I Peter 2:21

Jesus came to . . .

- Luke 19:10

Jesus came to . . .

5. Now go back through these reasons why Jesus became a man and personalize them for yourself. Work your own name into the sentence because Jesus came into the world to accomplish all of these things for you!

- John 1:18

Jesus came to . . .

- I John 3:8

Jesus came to . . .

- Hebrews 4:15; 5:1, 2

Jesus came to . . .

- I Peter 2:21

Jesus came to . . .

- Luke 19:10

Jesus came to . . .

6. The Magi (wise men) showed us what our response should be to Christ (see Matthew 2:11). How can you worship Christ in today's world?

KEEP In Mind

During Christmastime, have you ever seen the outdoor decoration that shows Santa Claus, with hat removed and head bowed, worshiping at the manger of the Christ Child? It is a magnificent statement about who we should focus on during Christmas.

The Magi worshiped the child Jesus. We, however, can worship the King Jesus, who is at the Father's side. And it is important to worship Christ throughout the year, not just at Christmas. Will you commit yourself to spend more time worshipping Jesus? Will you adore Him as the Lamb of God, and praise Him as the prophesied Messiah—God in a human body?

PRAY About It

Take time out to praise God by writing out a response to each of these phrases from John 1:14.

The Word became flesh and made his dwelling among us.

Response:

We have seen his glory

Response:

The glory of the One and Only

Response:

Who came from the Father

Response:

Full of grace and truth

Response:

Also keep track of your continuing prayer requests and answers to prayer.

WEEK 7 History's MVP

The Life of Jesus

1 World Series Madness

Fans packed out Yankee Stadium on October 18, 1977, to see the World Series. It was the New York Yankees versus the Los Angeles Dodgers. The Yankees were leading the series—3 games to 2. They needed a victory on this night to win it all, and they desperately wanted to do it on their home turf. But for that to happen, somebody would have to step forward and play the game of his life.

Somebody did.

In the fourth inning, right fielder Reggie Jackson stepped up to the plate and on the first pitch hammered a home run into the right field stands. The Yankees had the lead. The crowd went wild. The Dodgers changed pitchers.

In the fifth inning, Reggie again stepped into the batter's box, and on the first pitch sent another ball sailing into the right field stands. The Yanks were on their way. The fans went crazy. Again, the Dodgers changed pitchers.

Finally, in the bottom of the eighth, Reggie flexed his tree-trunk arms and crushed yet another first pitch over the center field wall—home run number three. The Yankees had their World Series. Pandemonium. The Dodgers went home.

Three pitchers. Three pitches. Three swings. Three home runs. One World Series title. For this, Reggie Jackson came to be known as "Mr. October." Needless to say, he was voted the series Most Valuable Player. Many people have played in the World Series. And many have won the MVP award. But nobody has ever done what Reggie Jackson did on that October night in Yankee Stadium.

Greatness is measured in various ways. In professional sports it is measured by one standard—performance. In wartime, greatness is measured by military strength and brilliant strategy. In life, greatness is measured by personal achievement or conduct, or service to other people. Throughout history, there have been many who have lived extraordinary lives. And many have given of themselves in service to society and country. But nobody in history has ever lived the kind of life Jesus Christ lived.

Take time to discover why Jesus Christ is history's Most Valuable Person.

2 His Words

There was something about what Jesus said and the way He spoke that caused people in His day to respond to Him.

1. Underline key words that show how people responded to Jesus. Circle the things that the people responded to.

Matthew 7:28, 29
When Jesus had finished saying these things, the crowds were amazed at his teaching, because he taught as one who had authority, and not as their teachers of the law.

John 7:46
"No one ever spoke the way this man does," the guards declared.

John 6:68
Simon Peter answered him, "Lord, to whom shall we go? You have the words of eternal life."

2. What did Christ Himself say about His words (Luke 21:33)?

3. What reason did Jesus give for His powerful teaching (John 8:38)?

Jesus spoke with authority and conviction because His message was one that met people's needs and changed their hearts. His words were powerful because they were true and because they came from God. He often spoke in simple, profound parables. Two thousand years later, His words are as life-changing now as they were when He first spoke them.

4. If Jesus' words were so powerful, why do you think you don't always find yourself amazed at His teaching?

3 His Works

Jesus went beyond talking a good talk. He backed up His words with astonishing displays of power. His powerful demonstrations were miracles—events for which there are no natural explanations.

Jesus had no peers when it comes to miracles—then or ever. But the wonder of His works was not just in the miraculous way He performed them, but also in the way He dealt with the people who benefitted from them.

1. What characterized Jesus' miracles (Mark 1:40, 41)?

2. What kinds of miracles did Jesus do?

SCRIPTURE	IDENTIFY MIRACLE
Matthew 9:2, 6, 7	
Luke 17:12-14	
Luke 7:11-16	
Mark 4:35-41	
John 6:2, 10, 11	
John 6:19	

3. When John the Baptist was in prison, and in need of assurance that Jesus was the Messiah, what message did Christ send Him (Luke 7:22)?

In other words, Jesus not only lived the most extraordinary life in history, but also the finest one. He did what no one else has done. He gave Himself to those in need. He was compassionate and caring. As the Master, He served His disciples (John 13:12-15). He loved the unlovely, the unloving, and the unlovable. And He lived this way consistently before every person He met, every day of His life, every moment of every day! Jesus is history's MVP.

4. Suppose Jesus came to your town today, and you were on the side of the road watching Him pass by. Would you ask Him for a miracle? If so, what would you ask for?

4 His Walk

But Jesus wasn't just a miracle worker. His life consisted of more than performing supernatural deeds. In fact, He was in many respects a normal Jewish boy.

1. What can you see in the verses below that tells you Jesus was like us in many ways?

- Luke 2:52
- Matthew 4:1
- Hebrews 4:15
- John 11:5, 35

2. But though He was like us in many ways, one thing separates Him from every other man who ever lived. What is it (I Peter 2:22; Hebrews 7:26)?

Jesus challenged anyone to find just one sin in Him, but they couldn't (John 8:46). Even His enemies were unable to find fault in Him (Luke 23:22, 47). He lived what He preached and preached what He lived.

3. But how does His sinless life relate practically to you today?

- Hebrews 2:17, 18
- John 16:33
- Philippians 4:13
- I John 4:4

4. In what area of temptation or sin do you need the Lord's help?

5 His Witness

We've looked at the powerful words Jesus spoke, the miraculous works He performed and the sinless walk He showed us. But how do we thread them all together in a way that makes sense? By looking at the impact He made.

1. Describe Jesus' impact on Peter.

- The old Peter (Matthew 26:69-74)

- The new Peter (Acts 2:14; 4:8-13)

2. Describe Jesus' impact on Paul.

- The old Paul (Acts 8:3; 9:1)

- The new Paul (Acts 17:2, 3)

3. Describe Jesus' impact on society.

- The early Christians (Acts 1:14; 17:6)

4. Describe Jesus' impact on you.

- I would describe the old me as . . . (support your answer with Scripture)

- But through Christ the new me is . . . (support your answer with Scripture)

5. What is happening in your life that would cause others to say the same thing about you?

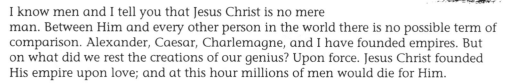

KEEP In Mind

Jesus' life had an immeasurable impact and influence that has changed the course of human history. Even our calendars are based on His life (B.C., A.D.). Look at what Napoleon Bonaparte said about the Savior:

> I know men and I tell you that Jesus Christ is no mere man. Between Him and every other person in the world there is no possible term of comparison. Alexander, Caesar, Charlemagne, and I have founded empires. But on what did we rest the creations of our genius? Upon force. Jesus Christ founded His empire upon love; and at this hour millions of men would die for Him.

Jesus shattered the status quo in His time. He changed the way people looked at the institutions of slavery and government, marriage and family. He elevated the status of women, and brought healing to the sick and hope to the hurting. He tore down the walls of prejudice and brought reconciliation between races. But best of all, He brought salvation to people. Today, His impact has not worn off. He is still changing society, healing hearts, and mending broken lives. As one famous essay put it:

> All the armies that ever marched, and all the navies that ever were built, and all the parliaments that ever sat, and all the kings that ever reigned, put together, have not affected the life of mankind on this earth as powerfully as has that one solitary life.

> Jesus spoke the greatest words—words of hope and salvation.
> Jesus performed the greatest works—works of healing and deliverance.
> Jesus lived the greatest life—a life of righteousness.
> Jesus left the greatest witness—a witness that impacted all of history.

1. As you look at the life of Jesus, what is one aspect of His life that you want to develop in your own?

2. What is one way you could accomplish this in your life?

PRAY **About It**

Finish this prayer.

Lord, I want to model my life after Yours, especially in . . .

Don't forget to keep track of your other prayer requests and answers.

WEEK ‹8› Paid in Full!

The Death of Jesus

1 Shadow of Death

In the City Museum and Art Gallery in Manchester, England, there hangs a powerful painting entitled "The Shadow of Death" by artist Holman Hunt. It was painted over a century ago while Hunt was on a three-year venture in the Holy Land. As he sat on the roof of his house in Jerusalem, he was moved to paint a most interesting portrait of Christ. The painting depicts Jesus as a young man working as a carpenter in Joseph's shop. The sun is setting in the western sky, and it's rays are shining through the open door. Jesus has risen from the workbench and is stretching out His tired arms. As He does this, the rays of the setting sun throw His shadow on the wall behind Him in the shape of a cross.

Some have said that the cross cast its long shadow on Jesus from the time He was born. He hammered away in Joseph's shop as a young man, but one day He would be hammered to a wooden cross. After all, the cross was the primary reason for His mission. He was born to die. And though Jesus had warned His disciples several times regarding His imminent death (Mark 8:31; 9:31; 10:32-34, 45), the reality of the cross did not hit home until the night before His crucifixion, while in the garden of Gethsemane.

As you complete this study, you will follow step-by-step the events leading up to the Crucifixion. And as you do, try to imagine yourself as one of the disciples, and prepare yourself to witness the greatest drama in recorded history.

2 Blood, Sweat, and Tears

You are in the garden of Gethsemene now. It is a few hundred yards from the eastern gate of the city of Jerusalem. After eating your last meal with Jesus, you sing a hymn together and then walk the short distance to the garden, a place you have been before with Jesus.

1. What do you see there (Mark 14:32-34)?

2. Why do you think Jesus felt this way (Mark 14:35, 36)?

3. What do you think the "cup" refers to, when Jesus asks God, if it's His will, to take the "cup" from Him (compare Hebrews 2:9)?

4. Just how bad did Jesus' sorrow and stress get (Luke 22:44)?

Jesus apparently experienced a rare medical condition known as "hematidrosis," where under enormous emotional stress, tiny blood vessels actually burst and mix with the sweat glands, here causing Jesus to literally sweat blood.

5. What added to His sadness and pain (Mark 14:39, 40)?

6. Think of one of the saddest, darkest moments in your life. How does it compare when you compare it to Jesus' pre-crucifixion hours?

Jesus was beginning to experience the weight of what lay ahead for Him. This depression and stress alone could have shut His body down had it not been for an angel sent to strengthen Him (Luke 22:43).

3 Silence of the Lamb

1. Who showed up to arrest Jesus (John 18:3)?

2. In the midnight darkness, they want to know which one is Jesus. The Lord identifies Himself and they all suddenly fall back on the ground (Jesus merely allowed a flash of His deity to shine forth for a brief second, letting them know His arrest would be voluntary). Even though He does not resist arrest, they tie Him up anyway and lead Him away to the first of six (mostly middle-of-the-night) trials (John 18:4-13). Three of these trials would be before the Jewish religious leaders, and three would be before the Roman officials. Let's get an overview of what happens at each of them.

THE RELIGIOUS TRIALS

Trial #1—Before Annas (John 18:12, 13, 19-23)

Annas, the influential former high priest, is the first to interrogate. The Lord is calm. (Annas knew it was illegal to hold court at night and to ask a witness to testify against himself.) Jesus is struck across the face. Annas orders Jesus to be taken to the acting high priest Caiaphas (John 18:24).

Trial #2—Before Caiaphas (Matthew 26:57-68; Mark 14:65)

Here, Caiaphas and the religious leaders (the Sanhedrin) hastily arrange a trial. Jesus openly declares that He is the Messiah. They unanimously call for His death and physically abuse him. It is around three a.m. Jesus will be held in Caiaphas's palace for about three more hours while the Jewish leaders come up with a plot to destroy Him.

Trial #3—Before Caiaphas (Matthew 27:1, 2)

It's daybreak now, about six a.m. Jesus is interrogated again, after which the high priest and the Sanhedrin officially issue the death penalty. Their only problem is that the Roman government will not allow the Jews to exercise capital punishment, so they take Jesus to Pilate.

THE ROMAN TRIALS

Trial #1—Before Pilate (Luke 23:1-7)

Pontius Pilate was the Roman governor of Judea and a fairly typical politician. He questions Jesus, who doesn't even defend Himself against the false charges leveled against Him. Convinced He is not guilty, Pilate decides the case is under Herod's jurisdiction.

Trial #2—Before Herod (Luke 23:8-12)

Herod, who had beheaded John the Baptist, had heard about Jesus. Although he questions Jesus at length, Jesus says nothing (I Peter 2:23). Herod wants to see Jesus perform a magic trick or miracle. But Jesus isn't about to become a court jester for Herod. So Herod puts a royal robe on Him and mocks Him, then sends Him back to Pilate.

Trial #3—Before Pilate (Luke 23:13-25)

Pilate thought he was through with Jesus and is not pleased to have to deal with Him again. Pilate tells the crowd that Jesus is innocent and tries to release Him. But the religious rulers and the angry mob remind Pilate of an annual Roman custom of releasing one prisoner. They demand that Pilate release a condemned criminal named Barabbas and let Jesus die in his place. After resisting, Pilate finally caves into their demands and sentences Jesus to die. Before the trial is officially over, Pilate punishes Jesus, thinking this will satisfy the crowd. He is wrong.

3. Why do you think these people hated Jesus so much (John 3:19, 20)?

4. According to Jesus, what did their actions mean (John 15:23)?

4 The Death of Deaths

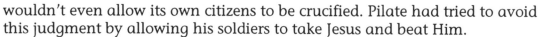

Peter has denied the Lord publicly. Judas has committed suicide.

Crucifixion was the worst of deaths. Developed by the Phoenicians and adopted by the Romans, it was a form of execution reserved for society's worst criminals. So inhumane was this form of death that Rome wouldn't even allow its own citizens to be crucified. Pilate had tried to avoid this judgment by allowing his soldiers to take Jesus and beat Him.

1. How is this beating described (John 19:1-3)?

Scourging was often done with a cat-of-nine-tails, which was like a bullwhip with nine leather straps protruding from the handle. At the end of each strap were imbedded sharpened pieces of bone and iron. This gave the whip weight on the ends. Many people died from the scourging alone. Here's why: With each swing, the cat-of-nine-tails would wrap around the person's torso. The razor-sharp ends would sink into the skin, tearing chunks of flesh from the person's body when the soldier would jerk the whip back.

The crown of thorns—two-to-three-inch, needle-like thorns—was forced down on Jesus' head, no doubt puncturing the skin. The soldiers draped a purple robe on Jesus and began to mock Him as a king. They spit on Him and beat Him in the face.

It's close to nine a.m. Jesus is marched through the city streets to a place called Golgotha, a rocky hill overlooking Jerusalem. Before they crucify Him, Jesus refuses to drink a narcotic painkiller offered to Him (Mark 15:23).

First, Jesus is stripped, which adds to the shame of being crucified. A spike is driven between the bones in His wrists. His knees are bent up toward His chest and one long spike is pounded through both His feet at the bottom of the ankles. The cross is hoisted up and dropped into a hole. Jesus' pain is excruciating. The weight of His body pulling down on His wrists causes Jesus to push up, which puts the weight on His ankles. His joints swell and His muscles burn with cramps.

Most crucified people died from suffocation after they no longer had the strength to push themselves up to draw air into their lungs. Some lingered on the cross for days. To quicken death, the soldiers would sometimes break the legs of the criminals, making it impossible for them to get air. Read John 19:33-37.

2. Why did Jesus go through this (John 15:13)?

5 It Is Finished!

Could anything be worse for Jesus than the physical pain on the cross? Absolutely.

1. What was taking place in the spiritual realm as Jesus hung on the cross (II Corinthians 5:21)?

God poured out His wrath against sin on Jesus. You could say that Jesus experienced an eternal dose of hell and judgment in a compacted six-hour period in His atoning sacrifice for our sin (I John 2:2). Think of it. Whatever pain hell involves, Jesus felt it.

But that's not all.

2. According to Matthew 27:46, what else did Jesus experience? Why do you think this was especially horrifying for Him?

3. As Jesus finished His work on the cross, what else was He accomplishing for us?

- Romans 5:1

- Ephesians 1:7

- Hebrews 7:25

4. Think back to the time that you first understood and accepted Christ's work on the cross. What happened? What did you experience? What impact did it have on you?

5. How different are your feelings about Christ's work on your behalf now? Have they dwindled in intensity? Are they more intense? Explain.

6. Do you see any need to rekindle your appreciation for Christ's suffering on your behalf? If so, how can you do this?

Consider that it cost seven million dollars to disassemble the London Bridge and transport it, stone by stone, from its original site on the Thames River to Lake Havasu City, Arizona, where it was reassembled.

The Golden Gate Bridge cost $35 million to build. And the San Francisco-Oakland Bay Bridge cost a whopping $77,200,000 to construct.

But the world's costliest bridge wasn't built with steel and cement. It was built with the body and blood of the Lord Jesus Christ. Through His death, He spanned the great gulf between us and God. He paid our sin debt in full. It is finished! If you're a Christian, you have been set free from sin and God's judgment—all because of the cross.

PRAY About It

When was the last time that you spent time thinking about Jesus' suffering on the cross? When was the last time that you thanked God for saving you? Set aside some time now to do it while this study is fresh in your mind. Write out your thoughts in the form of a prayer.

Lord, when I think about what You did on the cross for me, I . . .

Keep track of continuing prayer requests and answers.

WEEK 9 Gravebuster!

The Resurrection of Jesus

1 End of the Road

Funerals are strange events. Maybe you've attended one. You dress conservatively, ride in fancy cars, and see people you haven't seen in years. You shed tears, speak kind words, and share fond memories. Then you drive in a long procession of cars to the cemetery.

A famous or wealthy person's funeral is measured by the location of the cemetery plot, an expensive casket, and a "who's who" guest list. At the funeral of a president or a head of state, people from all over the world come to pay their respects. Sometimes the event is even televised. On the other hand, a poor person's funeral is marked by simplicity.

Matthew 27 devotes five verses to the preparation of Jesus' body for burial and the actual burial or, more accurately, entombment. Most of Matthew 27 focuses on Jesus' trial and crucifixion. The only recorded believers there to witness His death were the disciple John, Mary (Jesus' mother), and a few other courageous, faithful women. The remaining disciples were hiding out of fear for their lives and in mourning for their Lord. It was a dark day for them, and they were in no mood for a funeral.

As for the Pharisees, however, they had reason to celebrate. Their chief critic and competition was now silenced. No one would call them hypocrites anymore. They could now go back to their positions of honor and respect among the people—now that this Galilean dissident was out of the way.

Or was He?

2 God in the Graveyard

In his book, *The Passover Plot*, author Hugh Schonfield insisted Jesus faked His own death in order to fulfill Old Testament prophecies concerning the Messiah. Occasionally someone will come forward claiming Jesus didn't actually die on the cross—He just had a real bad fainting spell. Although critics and philosophers come and go, the fact remains—Jesus died on the cross. But what real evidence is there for us that He actually died?

1. How do these verses describe Jesus' death?

- Matthew 27:50

- John 19:32-35

- Mark 15:44, 45

When Jesus died, strange things happened, such as:

• The veil of the temple was torn in two from top to bottom (Matthew 27:51).

• The earth shook and rocks split (vs. 51).

• Tombs broke open and many believers who had died came back to life (vs. 52).

• The Roman centurion guarding Jesus confessed that He was the Son of God (vs. 54).

All this takes place after the sky had turned dark for three hours (Matthew 27:45). This was no ordinary death.

Jesus was dead, but the priests and Pharisees still weren't satisfied. They remembered Jesus' predictions of a resurrection. To prevent His disciples from stealing the body and claiming Jesus was alive again, they installed a custom-made Roman security system. How did they do it?

1. They secured the tomb with _____ (Matthew 27:65).

2. They secured the tomb with _____ (Matthew 27:66).

The tomb of Jesus was now officially secured, protected, and guarded with the authority of Caesar himself. Usually criminals are guarded before they are executed, not afterward! But no problem. Nothing was going to happen. Nothing could happen. Jesus was dead and gone. Right?

3 The Great Escape!

Ehrich Weiss was born in 1874 in Budapest, Hungary. At an early age he began performing card tricks in a dime museum. After developing his escape act, he changed his name to Harry Houdini and soon became a headliner, performing in many of the great theaters of the world.

People said he could escape just about anything—and he did—ten pairs of handcuffs, leg irons, ropes, chains, jail cells, nailed crates, underwater trunks, and straitjackets. No one could duplicate his amazing escapes.

Shortly before his death in 1926, he predicted he would come back from the dead exactly one year to the day of his death. So a year after he died, his widow held a seance to summon back the great escape artist. But Houdini didn't show up, so she held another seance a year later, and the year after that, but still no Houdini. To this day, on the anniversary of his death, curious parties gather to try once again to open the door for Houdini to come back from the dead. But Houdini is not coming back. Death is one trap from which no one escapes . . . unless you're the Son of God!

It's now early Sunday morning. Three women come to the tomb, bringing spices to anoint Jesus' body. They don't yet know about the soldiers, and wonder who will roll the huge boulder away from the entrance for them.

They are unaware that they are in for a sunrise surprise.

1. What happened before the women arrived at the tomb (Matthew 28:2-4)?

2. What happened to the guards?

3. What did the women discover (Mark 16:4-6)?

4. What did the angel tell them to do (Mark 16:7)?

5. Why do you think this was important?

Upon hearing the good news, Peter and John race to the tomb, where they find an empty grave (John 20:1-8). John believes Christ is alive and so they return to report the news to the others. Meanwhile, Jesus appears to Mary Magdalene, who runs to announce to the disciples that He's alive! And while all this is happening, the soldiers are relating their incredible experience to the chief priests, who, after counseling together, bribe them into saying the disciples stole the body while they were asleep (Matthew 28:11-15).

This unbelievable story was full of holes from the start. First, it is unlikely these cowardly disciples would attempt to take on the Roman government. They were too afraid to even come outside! Second, how could anyone roll a two ton boulder up an incline without waking the guards? And finally, how would the guards know it was the disciples who stole the body if they were asleep? Their story rates up there along with the tooth fairy and the Easter bunny!

The fact is, Jesus rose from the dead. He busted out of the grave. And the stone wasn't rolled away to let Him out, but rather to let us in! Jesus Christ is alive and at large today.

6. How does Acts 2:24 describe this event?

7. What emotions would you have felt if Jesus had appeared to you?

One of the reasons the disciples were excited was because they were beginning to realize some of the implications of Christ's resurrection. After all, what transformed them from wimpy cowards to the courageous men who changed the course of history? What changed Peter from being a weak witness who denied Christ into the powerful preacher who stood on the day of Pentecost and preached to thousands? What made each of these men willing to now go out and die for their faith? There's only one explanation: their Lord was alive again. Jesus Christ was resurrected!

4 Game Over . . . We Win!

One Easter while I was away at college (me, Jeff, the author), my girlfriend and I decided to attend a local church. It was a little more formal than what I was used to, but I knew I could still learn something, and besides, it was Easter. I figured even preachers who can't preach do well on Easter.

So we sat down and waded through the organ music until the minister finally stood up to deliver his message. About ten minutes into his sermonette He cleared his throat and said, "It's not really that important whether or not Christ actually rose from the dead. What's important was that He was alive in the minds of the disciples."

At those words, I woke up. My mouth went dry. Did I hear him correctly? I wanted to see the instant replay of that one. In fact, I wanted to stand up and say something! What he said frightened me. Here was a pastor who didn't even care if Jesus had actually risen from the dead! It made me want to know why my Lord's resurrection was so crucial to the Christian faith . . . and to my faith!

That sermon sent me digging into the Scriptures, and here's what I found:

A. The Promise of the Resurrection

- It was foretold in the Old Testament (Psalm 16:8-11; Isaiah 53:5-12).

- It was quoted in the New Testament (Acts 2:30-32; I Corinthians 15:4).

- It was foretold by Christ Himself (Mark 8:31; 9:9, 31; 10:33).

B. The Evidence of the Resurrection

Looking at I Corinthians 15:5-8, see how many eyewitnesses to Christ's resurrection you can find.

Jesus appeared to:

1.

2.

3.

4.

5.

Any court of law depends heavily on the testimony of eyewitnesses. Paul here puts these eyewitnesses on the stand to encourage us and to convince the world of the Resurrection.

1. Why would the above account be of help to those early Christians who never had the chance to see the resurrected Christ?

Anyone who can adequately explain away these appearances will explain away the Resurrection. But no one has because no one can!

C. The Consequences of the Resurrection

Just how important is the Resurrection? What does it mean? How does it make a difference in your life? Discover the following powerful implications for yourself from I Corinthians 15:14-19.

If Christ has not been raised, then

1.

2.

3.

4.

5.

6.

7.

Do you see how the Resurrection is the event on which Christianity stands or falls? It is the foundation of our faith. The cornerstone. The bedrock. The basis for our beliefs. It is the most significant event in history!

KEEP In Mind

The famous British General Wellington commanded the victorious forces at the battle of Waterloo that effectively ended the Napoleonic Wars. The story is told that when the battle was over, Wellington sent the great news of his victory back to England. A series of stations, each one within sight of the next, had been established to send coded messages between England and the continent. The message to be sent was, *Wellington defeated Napoleon at Waterloo*. But meanwhile a fog set in and interrupted the message sending. As a result, the only news people received was, *Wellington defeated*. Later, the fog cleared and the full message of victory became known. And all England rejoiced.

When Jesus died at the cross, He was victorious over sin and Satan. But the prince of darkness and all his demonic host actually thought they had won. As Jesus was laid in the ground, the only message the world could see was, *Jesus defeated*. But three days later the fog of the tomb lifted and the Lord came bursting out of death's cold grip. And ever since, the message has been clear, *Jesus defeated sin, Satan, and death*!!

Jesus took the sting out of death (I Corinthians 15:56). And if He has the power to conquer death, what does the Resurrection mean:

For your body (I Corinthians 15:42-44; 50-54)?

When you die (I Corinthians 15:54, 55)?

When you're tempted (I Corinthians 15:56, 57)?

In your service (I Corinthians 15:58)?

PRAY About It

Write out a prayer: Thank God that His resurrection power is available to you. Trust Him to give you that power each day. Allow the living Lord to live His life through you as you face life head on. Realize that through Christ's power, you can cope with whatever situation you face (Philippians 4:13).

Keep track of other continuing prayer requests and answers.

Who Do You Say That I Am?

The Deity of Jesus

1 I Am the Greatest

People who brag on themselves are usually either too proud or given to exaggeration, or both. And no one was better at bragging than former heavyweight boxing champ Muhammad Ali. He was the master of the overstatement. Granted, he was the greatest fighter of his day. In fact, his trademark slogan was, "I am the greatest!" Before his 1971 prize fight with Smokin' Joe Frazier, Ali was quoted by *Life* magazine as saying, "There seems to be some confusion. We're gonna clear this confusion up on March 8. We're gonna decide once and for all who is king! There's not a man alive who can whup me. I'm too smart. I'm too pretty. I am the greatest. I am the king! I should be a postage stamp—that's the only way I could get licked!"

On March 8, Ali got licked by Frazier.

On another occasion when Ali was flying first class, he was asked by the stewardess if he wanted something to drink. "Superman don't need no drink," came the champ's reply. Minutes later, she reminded him to fasten his seat belt for takeoff. He looked up at her and said, "Superman don't need no seat belt." Without batting an eye, the stewardess shot back, "Look, Superman don't need no airplane either. Now fasten your seat belt!"

Though he was a great fighter (and an even better entertainer), Muhammad Ali simply couldn't back up some of the incredible egocentric claims he made regarding himself.

But when we look at Jesus, we see a man who backed up every one of His claims with proof and evidence. He didn't leave anyone guessing about who He was. Put simply, Jesus Christ claimed to be more than man. He was God in the flesh.

Perhaps you've been in conversations where you wished you could explain to someone why you believe Jesus is God. Perhaps you've felt unprepared to defend your faith. Or you've been hit with the question, "Why do you Christians think your religion is the only right one?" Or, "How can you be so narrow-minded about God?" Perhaps you have wondered why we as Christians believe that Jesus is God.

This study will strengthen your faith and understanding about who Jesus was and is. It will help you more effectively share Christ with your friends and will challenge you to apply His Lordship in every area of your life. We'll do this by tackling tough questions about Jesus' claims.

2 What Did Jesus Claim?

1. What did Jesus say to make the Pharisees so hopping mad that they felt murderous (John 10:28, 30-33)?

Jesus made direct claims to be God. In fact, He also made a series of I AM statements, such as:

    I am (John 6:35) . . .

    I am (John 8:12) . . .

I am (John 10:7) . . .

I am (John 10:11, 14) . . .

I am (John 11:25) . . .

I am (John 14:6) . . .

I am (John 15:5) . . .

and His simple, yet profound, claim,

I AM (John 8:54-59; compare Exodus 3:14)

2. What happens to people today who claim to be God?

3 Did He Prove His Claims Were True?

The story is told that French artist Paul Gustave Doré lost his passport while traveling in a foreign country. When he arrived at the international border, he explained his dilemma to the immigration officer and assured him he was Doré, the well-known painter. The official calmly handed him a piece of paper and simply said, "Prove it!" Within a few minutes Doré produced a brilliant sketch that fully convinced the official of who he was.

1. What evidence did Jesus produce to show that He was God?

• Mark 2:5-12

• Matthew 14:25-33

2. The miraculous events (miracles) surrounding the life and ministry of Christ were His way of proving to the world He was exactly who He said He was. Finish these sentences:

√ When the Pharisees needed proof Jesus had the authority to forgive the sins of the lame man, Jesus (Mark 2:5-12) . . .

√ When His disciples needed proof He was in control of all things, Jesus (Mark 4:35-41) . . .

√ When the multitudes needed proof that the one they were following was indeed the Son of God, Jesus (John 6:1-15) . . .

√ When the world needed proof that Jesus was who He claimed to be, God (John 2:18-22; Romans 1:4) . . .

Hey, what more evidence could anyone want?

3. Can you think of why someone wouldn't be convinced?

4 Who Knew Jesus Best?

Nobody knows you like your family. They see you early in the morning (bad breath) and late at night (tired and grumpy). They see you in all kinds of moods and in all types of situations. They see your good traits as well as your warts. If anyone could give an accurate description of what you're really like, it would be your family because they live with you.

What about those who knew Jesus best? What about the ones who lived with Him night and day? What about others who were associated with Him? They would obviously know Him best. What were their conclusions about Jesus?

- John the Baptist (John 1:29, 30, 34)

- Thomas (John 20:27, 28)

- James, the brother of Jesus (Galatians 1:19; James 2:1)

- Paul (Philippians 2:6, 7; Colossians 1:15-19; 2:9) (Paul refers to Jesus as Lord about 200 times!)

- Peter (Matthew 16:15-17)

- Stephen (Acts 7:59)

- John (John 1:1)

These men were in a position to know Christ better than anyone else. And they were thoroughly convinced Jesus was exactly who He said He was. It is unlikely these men would then go out and die for a truth they didn't really believe. In short, Jesus' companions say He is God.

5 What Do You Say?

It was the young lawyer's first day on the job in his brand new office when there was a knock on his open door. Thinking it is a prospective client, he decides to look busy, so he picks up the phone and starts talking: "Look, Harry, about that amalgamation deal. I think I better run down to the factory and handle it personally. Yes. . . . No. I don't think $3 million will swing it. We better have Rogers from Seattle fly down to meet us here. . . . OK. I'll call you back later."

He then looks up at the prospective client and says, "Good morning, may I help you?" The man says, "No sir. You can't help me at all. I'm just here to hook up your phone."

Unlike this fellow, Jesus wasn't pretending to be great. He was and is great.

His birth says He is God.

His sinless life says He is God.

His miraculous deeds say He is God.

His direct claims say He is God.

His indirect claims say He is God.

His sacrificial death says He is God.

His powerful resurrection says He is God.

His supernatural ascension says He is God.

His closest followers say He is God.

All of Scripture says He is God.

The early church says He is God.

History affirms He is God.

Changed lives confirm He is God.

Isn't that exciting to know your Savior is not a philosophy, or an idea, or a religion or some mysterious force, but God Himself in human packaging? That's something to shout about!

So, how would you answer those two questions asked earlier? "Why do you Christians know your religion is the only right one?" and "How can you be so narrow-minded about God?"

Along Highway 10 in Louisiana stands a large billboard that catches everyone's eye. It stands high above the ground near the Mississippi River bridge. On it is a picture of Jesus Christ hanging on the cross, head bowed. The caption underneath says: "It's your move!"

Recognizing who Jesus is always produces a response, even for Christians. So now it's your move.

After learning the truths in this chapter, do you see a need to respond differently to His deity than you have in the past? How?

How can you better obey these commands? Be specific.

- Matthew 22:37

- John 14:15

PRAY About It

During your prayer time, ask God to make real to you the truth of Colossians 2:9 and to reveal to you any shortsightedness concerning the deity of Christ.

You could also write out a prayer in the form of an acrostic in which you acknowledge Jesus as Lord and God. If you want, use the word DEITY as the foundation for your acrostic prayer. (Write out other general prayer requests and their answers.)

D

E

I

T

Y

UNIT Three

God the Holy Spirit

Now you've come to the person of the Trinity who probably can help you the most—but whom most people know the least—in your quest to grow closer to God.

That's right—the Holy Spirit.

Jesus Himself said that the Holy Spirit was for our good and would help give us the mind of Christ (John 16:7; 14:26).

Yet for the most part, people are more familiar with God the Father and Jesus than the Holy Spirit.

But not anymore.

In this unit, you will learn about who the Holy Spirit is and His presence and ministry in your life. You will also learn about some special gifts and Christian temperaments (better known as "fruit") the Spirit can help develop in your own life.

But most of all, you will feel closer to this person whom Jesus calls "the Counselor." Get to know Him, and let Him give you counsel in your life.

WEEK ◄11 He's Holy, But He's No Ghost!

The Person of the Spirit

1 Spiritual Mist

Some people have referred to the Holy Spirit as if He were an impersonal force or power. Others have called Him a ghost, which tends to conjure up images of spiritual mist or spooky vapor. People sometimes think of Him as similiar to one of the special effects apparitions from the movie *Ghostbusters*! Christians refer to Him as the third Person of the Trinity. But what does that mean? What are we saying when we say the Holy Spirit is a Person?

Perhaps some of the misunderstanding about the Holy Spirit is because we have a hard time picturing Him. It is easier to relate to and picture Jesus. We think of Jesus as a baby, a child, a young carpenter, a miracle worker, a Savior dying on the cross, a resurrected Christ. But the Holy Spirit is spirit and you can't see Him. Who is He? What does He do? How are we to relate to Him? Let's find out.

1. Lots of movies have been made about ghosts. Name as many of them as you can think of. Then write one sentence descriptions about them. Contrast them to what you think of the Holy Spirit.

MOVIE 1:

MOVIE 2:

MOVIE 3:

2 Person to Person

You may be surprised to find out how many specific details there are about the Holy Spirit in the Scriptures. Here are a few reasons why Christians refer to the Holy Spirit as the third Person of the Trinity. The key thought here is "Person."

• A Person Has Intellect

1. How do these verses show that the Holy Spirit has intellect (I Corinthians 2:10-13)?

• A Person Has Emotion

2. What emotion is identified here and what causes it (Ephesians 4:29-32)?

3. What emotion is identified here (Romans 15:30)?

4. List a few of the emotions you feel from time to time. Do you think the Holy Spirit feels any of these as well? If so, which ones?

• **A Person Has a Will**

5. In what circumstances do these Scriptures show the Holy Spirit exercising His will (I Corinthians 12:11; Acts 16:7)?

The Holy Spirit has the mind of God. His emotions can be grieved and quenched (I Thessalonians 5:19). And He chooses to work as He wills. Put these all together and you have a Person, the Person of the Holy Spirit. He's more than a name on a Bible page. He's as real as Jesus and God the Father are. But there is an even deeper facet of the Holy Spirit.

3 Another Counselor

To say the Holy Spirit is equal to God is to say He possesses all the same attributes and characteristics of God. But does the Bible teach that?

The Spirit is equal with _____ (John 14:16, 17).

The Spirit is equal with _____ (Acts 5:3, 4).

The Spirit can also be sinned against like God (Matthew 12:31, 32).

The following verses show that the Holy Spirit shares God's characteristics. What are these characteristics?

• Psalm 139:7

• Hebrews 9:14

• I Corinthians 2:11

So the Holy Spirit is equal to God because of who He is. But we also know He is God because He has done the things only God can do. What are some of them?

He _____ by His power (Romans 8:2, 11).

He was involved in _____ (Genesis 1:2).

He _____ Scripture (II Peter 1:21).

He was instrumental in _____ (Luke 1:35).

Put simply, the Holy Spirit is fully God. He is co-equal and co-eternal with God the Father and God the Son. This is what Christians call the Trinity. That word sounds religious, but exactly what does it mean?

4 Three in One

This is your Brain.

This is your Brain trying to figure out the Trinity.

The Bible clearly teaches there is only one God (Deuteronomy. 6:4, 5) and that He exists in three Persons—the Father, Son, and Spirit (now we're getting into some mystery, so hang on!). We refer to the three members of the Godhead as the Trinity. That is part of God we cannot fully understand. Someone once said that the person who tries to understand the Trinity with his mind will soon go out of his mind! Trying to figure out the Trinity is like trying to put the Atlantic Ocean into a Dixie cup! Even so, there are aspects of the Trinity we can understand. And part of that is knowing what the Trinity is not.

• The Trinity is not three roles (Father, Son, Spirit) played by one Person. It's not like saying you're a son, a student, and a musician—three roles, one person. The Trinity is not one God who wears three hats. Jesus referred to the Father and the Spirit as being distinct Persons (John 8:49; 14:16, 17). Three Persons; One God.

• The Trinity is not three separate gods functioning together like a team. Wrong answer. That would be what theologians call polytheism, or believing in many gods. God is One (Deuteronomy. 6:4, 5). Three Persons; One God.

• The Trinity is not three members, each of which is one-third God, but together They become 100 percent God. Negative. We have already seen that each member of the Godhead is fully God. Three Persons; One God.

One God exists in three Persons. This is the Tri-unity of God, the Trinity.

Do we fully understand it? No.

Is that okay? Yes.

Although the word Trinity isn't found in the Bible, the truth of it is taught in the Scripture. In what way do you see the Trinity in these verses?

- Matthew 28:19

- II Corinthians 13:14

- Ephesians 4:4-6

- Titus 3:4-6

The Holy Spirit is a Person, not an it. He is fully God and equal to the Father and the Son.

Earlier you read that Jesus promised He would send another Counselor to be with the disciples. This Counselor would be with them just as Christ was. He would now be the member of the Godhead who would primarily minister in the lives of Christians. If that is true, then we need to find out these kinds of questions. Check off any that particularly intrigue you and keep an eye out for the answers in future studies. Add any question you have that is not included in this list.

- Why did the Holy Spirit come?
- When did He officially get here?
- How does His ministry differ from that of Christ's?
- Why do I need the Holy Spirit?
- What has He done for me?
- What are His ministries in my life?
- What should I believe about Him?
- How am I supposed to relate to Him?

You'll discover the answer to these questions and more in the next few chapters. And you'll find that the Spirit's ministry in, to, and through you is the key to living a successful Christian life.

PRAY About It

Does anything about this Holy Spirit business confuse you? Ask God to make His truth clear to you throughout this study on the Spirit. Scripture encourages you to ask God for wisdom, and the request certainly seems justified here. Don't forget to keep track of continuing prayer requests and answers.

WEEK 12 Fire from Heaven!

The Coming of the Spirit

1 Extra-Special Gift

In a national mail-order magazine, the following gifts were offered for the birthday of that special someone in your life:

- His and Her Lear Jets
- His and Her llamas
- A trip around the world
- A diamond-studded putter for the golfer who has everything
- Dinner with your favorite celebrity
- An island in the Caribbean
- A fantasy sports camp where you can play with the pros
- A gas-powered turtleneck sweater (just kidding!)

Hey, if you're giving people llamas for their birthdays, you definitely have more money than sense. The point, of course, was to give the person the most expensive, extravagant gift imaginable (and you thought you were splurging when you bought your dad a tie!).

When God decided to celebrate the birthday of Christ's church, He did it by sending a very special gift to us—the Holy Spirit. It happened on a day that coincided with a Jewish feast called the Feast of Weeks, or Pentecost. Tens of thousands of Jews were in Jerusalem for this occasion. The streets were buzzing with activity. The marketplace and temple courts were packed like sardines with traveling visitors. And the disciples—they were off in an obscure second floor room—praying. But they wouldn't be there for long.

In this study, you will learn how, when, and why the Holy Spirit came to us.

2 The Promise-Keeper

Someone has said that promises are like pie crusts—easily made and easily broken. Politicians make promises. So do busy dads. Husbands and wives make a promise to one another too. And while some promises are broken, others are actually kept. Amazingly enough, there are even promises that are never taken advantage of. These promises are like unused gift certificates—no good until they're cashed in.

Such was the case with Crowfoot, the great chief of the Blackfoot Indians in southern Alberta. The story goes that he gave the Canadian Pacific Railroad permission to cross Blackfoot land. In return, he was given a lifetime railroad pass and the freedom to use any train at any time for any reason. It was the railroad's version of the blank check. Crowfoot put the pass in a leather case around his neck and, as far as we know, walked around for the rest of his life (maybe that's why they called him Crowfoot). There is no record he ever made use of his pass on any train. He never cashed in.

1. List some promises that have been made to you—both ones that were kept and ones that were broken.

KEPT   **BROKEN**

2. Jesus Christ, the ultimate Promise-Keeper, made a promise to His disciples. What was it (John 14:16, 17)?

John 14:16, 17
And I will ask the Father, and he will give you another Counselor to be with you forever—the Spirit of truth. The world cannot accept him, because it neither sees him nor knows him. But you know him, for he lives with you and will be in you.

The disciples decided to cash in on that promise, and so about 120 of them went to an upper room, where they waited and prayed (Acts 1:12-14).

3. What was one advantage of having Jesus go to heaven and the Holy Spirit come to earth (John 14:12)?

4. What would the Holy Spirit be able to do that Christ was unable to do?

Jesus had made many promises to His disciples over the three years they had been together, and He had kept them all. But there were several that were not yet fulfilled. He told them the Holy Spirit would fulfill some of these. Others would be fulfilled by Christ Himself later (John 14:1-3). But the disciples knew Jesus would send the Spirit. His word could be trusted.

5. Think of a time when someone broke a promise made to you. How did it make you feel toward that person?

6. But how does it make you feel knowing that Jesus has a perfect record of unbroken promises?

So the promise was made. The disciples were praying. Now let's see how the Spirit was given.

3 The Hour of Power

Something brought about a dramatic change in the lives of the disciples after Jesus' death. That something was a Someone—the Holy Spirit. He transformed a bunch of frightened, confused disciples into dynamic communicators of the Gospel, who also lived what they preached.

Here is what happened: After Jesus' resurrection, He spent forty days teaching and appearing to His disciples (Acts 1:3). Then Jesus ascended to the Father. A week later, the disciples, after praying in the upper room, went to the temple area to join the thousands gathered there for the celebration (Acts 2:4-6, 14, 41). They were in an upper room when something strange happened.

1. How is the Holy Spirit described (Acts 2:1-4)?

What connection do these verses have with Acts 2:1-4?

- John 3:8

- John 7:39

- Leviticus 9:24

The Spirit came to earth and gave evidence of His presence with power! Here, the disciples were supernaturally enabled to speak in foreign languages they had not previously learned!

2. Why do you think God was doing this (Acts 2:8-11)?

3. According to Jesus, what would be the purpose of this display of power (Acts 1:8)?

4. What do you suppose are "the wonders of God" referred to in Acts 2:11?

Through the power of the Holy Spirit, the disciples proclaimed the Gospel to people from all over the known world without even leaving Jerusalem! What an opportunity! God knew this would be a great time to inaugurate the church worldwide. That way, each new convert would take the Good News back with him to his own region. Christianity would now spread to virtually every region of the world. All this took place because of what happened at Pentecost!

When the Holy Spirit came, He did so to give you the power to be a witness for Jesus Christ.

5. When did Jesus say His followers would receive this power (Acts 1:8)?

6. In what sense do you need power to be His witness?

4 Your Heart, His Home

1. When Jesus made His promise to send the Holy Spirit to us, He said our relationship to Him would be different from that of previous believers. What would that difference be (John 14:17b, 20)?

2. How does Paul describe this (I Corinthians 6:19)?

After a church fire had destroyed the sanctuary, a neighbor expressed her concern to the pastor's wife. "I'm so sorry you lost your church," she said. "Oh, that's okay," replied the pastor's wife. "Our church is still here. We just lost our meeting place."

God doesn't live in the sanctuary of the local church. He lives in the hearts of His people. As a Christian, you have a special relationship with God the Holy Spirit. He dwells inside of you. He has made His home in your heart!

3. Do all Christians have the Holy Spirit in them (Romans 8:9, 11)?

4. If someone does not have the Spirit, what does that mean?

5. When does the Holy Spirit come to live in you (Acts 5:32)?

6. What does "obey" mean in Acts 5:32? See Acts 6:7. Compare Hebrews 4:6 with Hebrews 4:2.

7. What are some of the benefits of having God's presence?

- Deuteronomy 31:6

- Psalm 21:6

Before Pentecost, the Spirit was with believers and would come upon individuals for special tasks (Judges 14:19; I Samuel 10:9, 10). But after Pentecost our relationship with the Spirit became an internal dwelling. There is nothing that will cause Him to leave you (note the word "never" in Hebrews 13:5).

8. Has there ever been a time when you felt like God had left you, or like He was far away? If so, what did it feel like?

9. What two evidences do you have that the Holy Spirit will stay in you (John 14:15-18, 23; Romans 8:16)?

The Holy Spirit is:

- personal, so GET CLOSE TO HIM,
- powerful, so USE HIS POWER,
- permanent, so ENJOY HIS PRESENCE!

What a Gift!

PRAY About It

Write a prayer of thanks to God for sending the Holy Spirit. You may want to use the word SPIRIT as an acrostic for your prayer. Also keep track of other prayer requests and praise.

S

P

I

R

I

T

The Ministry of the Spirit

1 Great Explorers

When you think of the great explorers in history, familiar names come to mind—Christopher Columbus, Ponce de Leon, Vasco Balboa, Captain Cook, Admiral Byrd, Jacobus Jonker, Neil Armstrong . . . wait a minute—Jacobus Jonker? Who was he? What did he do?

Well, Mr. Jonker didn't explore the moon or the North Pole—he explored his own backyard! Yep. After each rain, ol' Jacobus would walk around in the mud on his small farm in South Africa. One day in the 1930s, he was sloshing around when he discovered something in the mud about the size of a golf ball. He went home, washed it off, then took it to the city where he discovered he had stumbled onto a 726-carat diamond! But Jacobus was no dummy, and neither was Mrs. Jonker. They sold their diamond and walked away with a cool $315,000.00! That's not bad, especially for the 1930s.

Sometimes Bible study can be like that. When you browse listlessly and with disinterest, you might miss something of great value. But if you stop long enough to carefully examine it, you will discover valuable spiritual diamonds.

Think of this chapter as a 726-carat diamond. You'll gather eight priceless truths.

You learned in the last chapter that the Holy Spirit came to live in you at the moment you trusted Christ for salvation. But He didn't just come to be your constant companion. He came to minister to you in several important ways.

2 God's Advance Plan

By the time then Vice President Bush came to Little Rock to campaign for his 1988 presidential bid, scores of Secret Service agents had already been there for weeks. They had spent days securing street routes, installing phone lines, meeting with key people, and eliminating any possible chance of a tragic mishap. On the day Bush arrived downtown, government agents were stationed on the roof of every building and in strategic windows, each of them scanning the crowd though binoculars and armed with high-powered rifles. They even mingled with the crowd (all this for a one-hour visit)! The Vice President's safety had been secured by his advance team.

In a similar way, the Holy Spirit was at work in your life long before you were saved. He spent years preparing your heart for that day in your life when you would say yes to Christ.

1. What was the Holy Spirit's ministry to you before you became a Christian (John 16:8)?

John 16:8
When he comes, he will convict the world of guilt in regard to sin and
righteousness and judgment.

2. What does it mean in our day to be convicted of something?

3. According to verses 8-11, what three things does the Holy Spirit convict you of?

    a. Your own:

    b. Jesus':

    c. The future _____ awaiting Satan and all unbelievers.

In other words, the Holy Spirit convinces us we are truly sinners, Christ is the Righteous One, and that there is a judgment for those who reject God's offer of salvation. That conviction makes our hearts ready to trust Christ because it causes us to feel our need for Him. In fact, without this ministry of the Spirit, none of us would ever be saved (Romans 3:10-12)! The result of this ministry is that we are brought to Christ.

3 I Didn't Feel a Thing

You may remember feeling the conviction of the Holy Spirit before you were saved, but you probably don't recall feeling the next three ministries of the Spirit. As you think back to the time you were saved (you may not remember the exact day—that's okay), there's a good chance you didn't have a spine-tingling experience, or sprout angel's wings. That's because this part of the Spirit's ministry to you is behind the scenes, unnoticed, unseen. It's like celebrating an important birthday—you don't necessarily feel older—but you are!

There are three ministries of the Spirit that occurred at the same time you became a Christian. That's when the Spirit gave you:

- **A New Beginning**

1. How is this ministry pictured in the New Testament (John 1:13; 3:3-7; Titus 3:5)? (Theologians call this regeneration.)

2. What is the practical result of this ministry (II Corinthians 5:17)?

3. What changes did Christ make in you that show you have a new life?

- **A New Identity**

4. How does Romans 8:14, 16 and Ephesians 2:19 describe this new identity?

- **A New Assurance**

5. How does Paul define this ministry of the Spirit (Ephesians 1:13; 4:30)?

6. What comes to your mind when you think of something being sealed?

There are three awesome results of being sealed with the Holy Spirit. Sealing was an ancient custom. It happened like this: when a king would send an important document, it would be rolled up and stamped with a wax seal, usually with the impression of the king's ring pressed into the wax. Anyone who saw that seal automatically knew three things:

1. This document belongs to the king. That's ownership. The seal would function like a monogram on a shirt or a book imprint inside the cover. It shows who owns it.

2. It is an authentic government document. That's authenticity. Like a registered art print, it proves the genuineness of the document.

3. It is protected by the authority of the king. That's security. Like registered mail, you don't tamper with it unless it is addressed to you. It's protected by the government.

So what does the Spirit do for you by sealing you?

1. It proves you belong to Him. He is responsible to care for you.

2. It proves you are a bona fide Christian. God says you're authentic. You're one of His original masterpieces (Ephesians 2:10). Because of Christ, God's seal of approval is on you.

3. You are divinely protected by the authority of heaven!

4 Gettin' Down to the Nitty-Gritty

We've looked at the ministry of the Spirit in our lives before we trusted Christ as well as His ministry at the moment of our salvation. But what about now? What does He do for us after we come to Christ?

What makes the next four ministries of the Spirit different from the rest is that they can happen every day . . . including today! The past ministries we've looked at happened without realizing it. But we actually have a say-so concerning these next four. To a certain degree, you decide how much of these you experience from day to day as you yield yourself to the Spirit's control.

Each day, the Spirit gives you:

- **A New Direction**

1. What does the Spirit do for you (Romans 8:14; Galatians 5:18)?

2. Do you feel you need this ministry for your life? Why or why not?

• A New Understanding

3. What other role does the Holy Spirit play in your life (John 16:12-15)?

4. In what way is this different from general guidance we just saw?

5. Complete this sentence:
The Holy Spirit helps me to:

6. Why is this particular ministry so important for you?

• A New Closeness

7. How does He accomplish this (Romans 8:26)?

Have you ever noticed that when people have difficulty communicating with someone who speaks a different language, they often speak slower and louder—as if that helps them understand better! Where's the bathroom? becomes

W H E R E ' S   T H E   B A T H R O O M ?

Sometimes you even end up saying the wrong thing. Once, while in Mexico, a young man tried to apologize and thought he said in Spanish, "I am embarrassed." Instead, he discovered that he had said, "I am pregnant."

Wouldn't it be great to have an interpreter, someone who could translate anything you said into the appropriate language? Guess what? You do! The Holy

Spirit is your interpreter before God! When you are praying, and can't seem to find the words to express what your heart really feels, He takes your thoughts and feelings and expresses them to God perfectly.

8. How could this bring you closer to God and encourage you to pray?

• A New Motivation

This ministry of the Holy Spirit is found in the first few words of John 16:14.

9. What is the Holy Spirit's role in your life here and what is one way the Holy Spirit could make this happen?

10. How do you think John 16:14 relates to what John the Baptist said in John 3:30?

So the Holy Spirit continually points us to Jesus. He doesn't focus on Himself. His ministry is to get us to keep looking at Jesus.

The Spirit's Ministry at a Glance

The Spirit's ministry in my life is:	Which gives me:	Resulting in:
Conviction	A new realization of sin	Bringing you to Christ
Regeneration	A new beginning	A changed person
Sealing	A new assurance	Confident in salvation
Guidance	A new direction	Not missing God's will
Illumination	A new understanding	Knowing God's Word
Intercession	A new closeness	More prayer
Glorification	A new motivation	Lifting up Jesus

Take a look at the results column. Which results do you think you most need in your life right now? Why?

PRAY About It

Write out a prayer concerning each of the following three areas and the role of the Holy Spirit in each area.

- Your growth as a believer

- Telling others about Christ

- Glorifying Christ

WEEK <14> Unwrapping Your Gift

The Gifts of the Spirit

1 What a Tour!

The youth choir tour was a huge success. It had traveled over two thousand miles throughout the southeastern U.S., performing at various churches. Now the choir was on its way home. After performing a final concert in its home church, the choir received a standing ovation. Following the concert, John, a senior who played the piano for the choir, mingled (as usual) with the congregation in the hopes of finding someone to witness to. About this time, a dear elderly woman came up to him.

"Young man," she said, "You are so talented on that piano. I believe the Lord has given you the spiritual gift of music." That comment stuck with John. No one had ever said that to him before. So before going to bed that night, John opened his Bible and looked up the word music. But he didn't find anything about the gift of music. Then he turned to the passages on spiritual gifts, but no gift of music there, either.

"But if I don't have the gift of music, what gift do I have?" he wondered. "Or do I even have one?" All John knew was that he loved to see people become Christians after the concerts. Confused and tired, John went off to sleep.

What help could you give John? Is there a spiritual gift of music? Or is playing the piano just a talent or a skill—like being funny or athletic or artistic? John's dilemma is not that uncommon among Christian students. Maybe you've felt like John. You've wondered whether or not you even have a spiritual gift.

Among high school students, the topic of spiritual gifts is not usually one of the most requested Bible studies. One reason for this may be because many Christians just don't know much about the subject. And when you think about it, why should they? What is so special about spiritual gifts? What are they? What purpose do spiritual gifts serve? Does every Christian have one? Do you have one? or two? or three?! And how do you know which one(s) you have? What do you do with it once you discover it? Can it be developed and strengthened? Can you lose it? And how do you use it?

2 God's Carpentry Shop

Spiritual gifts are like tools in a carpenter's shop—each one has a different purpose, a different use. One cuts; another hammers. One planes while another sands. One measures; another drills. But though each tool is different, in the end there is a finished product that reflects the beauty of each tool working together.

Like those tools, spiritual gifts are different, individual, diverse, but working toward a common good and a shared goal.

1. According to I Corinthians 12:8-11, where do spiritual gifts come from?

2. Who receives these spiritual gifts (I Corinthians 12:7; see also Ephesians 4:7)?

Though Scripture is not specific at this point, spiritual gifts may be given at the moment of salvation, since they are given to every believer. God also may take some ability that has been present all along and re-channel it for His usage. The verses above do not say that the Spirit gives gifts to only mature believers, but simply to every believer, without mention of spiritual maturity. This had to be the case here, for the Corinthian church was the most immature, worldly church in the New Testament, even though it was apparently the most gifted (I Corinthians 1:7). So having a spiritual gift has nothing directly to do with being a mature Christian. And God will never take back your spiritual gift from you (Romans 11:29). It's a gift!

3. On what basis does the Spirit decide which gift to give to whom (I Corinthians 12:11, 18)?

4. What exactly is the purpose of your spiritual gift (I Corinthians 12:7)?

Your spiritual gift was given to you so you could edify (or build up) other Christians. So you can look at spiritual gifts as tools to build with—only you don't build things—you build people. And as you exercise your gift, you will be built up too!

5. Describe a time when someone used his or her spiritual gift to build you up.

So the Holy Spirit, as He desires, gives every Christian a spiritual gift. And the purpose is to build up the body of Christ. You're a gifted person!

But what are the gifts?

3 Body Language

People communicate in different ways—verbally, nonverbally, through music or (like now) through writing. But another form of communication is through body language, such as slouching, giving a thumbs up, etc.

The Bible teaches that we are all important body parts in the body of Christ. And we communicate with our own form of body language. We do this when we use our spiritual gifts. When we build others up with our gifts, we are saying "I love you; you're important; and I need you" to our brothers and sisters in Christ.

So just what are the spiritual gifts mentioned in the Bible? And what do they mean? As you search the New Testament, you find there are basically five lists of gifts found. List them here:

Romans 12:6-8
(7 gifts)

_____

_____

_____

_____

_____

_____

I Corinthians 12:6-10
(9 gifts)

_____

_____

_____

_____

_____

_____

_____

_____

I Corinthians 12:28-30
(8 gifts)

_____

_____

_____

_____

_____

_____

Ephesians 4:11 (4 gifts)

_____

_____

_____

_____

I Peter 4:11 (2 gifts)

_____

_____

When we compare these lists with one another, we find there are eighteen spiritual gifts listed. We can better understand these gifts by dividing them into three major categories:

SPECTACULAR GIFTS   SPEAKING GIFTS   SERVING GIFTS

PANORAMIC
VIEW OF THE GIFTS

SPECTACULAR GIFTS—Intended to confirm the message of the apostles and accompanied by supernatural activity (Acts 2:22; Hebrews 2:3, 4). Such gifts include:

▶ **Healing**—(I Corinthians 12:9)—The ability to heal disease, miraculously, instantaneously (Mark 1:42), completely, and permanently (Matthew 14:36). Healing was done at the discretion of the one with the gift and did not always depend on the faith of the one being healed (John 9:25).

▶ **Miraculous Powers**—(I Corinthians 12:10)—The ability to do miracles in general. See Acts 5:9-11; 13:8-11.

▶ **Tongues**— I Corinthians 12:10)—The ability to speak in a known language not previously learned (Acts 2:4-6). This would be like all of a sudden finding yourself speaking the Gospel in fluent Arabic to an Arab! Paul told the Corinthians they were allowed to use this gift in church only if there was an interpreter (I Corinthians 14:27, 28).

▶ **Interpretation of Tongues**—(I Corinthians 12:10)—Used in the church service so that those not speaking the language could understand.

▶ **Faith**—(I Corinthians 12:9)—The ability to trust God for what appears impossible. He or she dreams great dreams and attempts great things for God, believing they will come to pass. This gift probably functions similarly to "mountain-moving" faith (Mark 11:22-24).

Various churches differ over whether the first group of gifts is still valid today. You may want to find out if your church takes a stance on this particular issue.

SPEAKING GIFTS—God used this set of gifts to further the message of the Gospel. Here is a list of these gifts:

▶**Apostleship**—(Ephesians 4:11)—Ordinarily, an apostle was someone who had been with the Lord from His baptism through His resurrection (Acts 1:21, 22). Each apostle had been a witness of the resurrected Christ (Acts 1:2, 3; I Corinthians 15:7, 8; Galatians 1:12). Apostles also spoke with great authority by direct revelation from God. This gift was an essential part of the foundation of the church (Ephesians 2:20).

▶ **Prophecy**—(I Corinthians 13:2; 14:29-32)—Refers to the ability to receive direct revelation from God and speak it to the church. The true prophet was always 100 percent correct when he spoke because he was speaking directly from God. Many today would classify preaching as "prophecy"—that is, conveying God's message to people.

▶ **Message of Wisdom**—(I Corinthians 12:8)—The ability to receive, know, and speak the wisdom of God.

▶ **Message of Knowledge**—(I Corinthians 12:8)—Includes the capacity to understand and communicate a message from God.

▶ **Distinguishing Spirits**—(I Corinthians 12:10)—All believers are to determine whether or not messages and experiences have a divine or demonic source (I John 4:1-6). Some believers may possess this ability in a special and heightened sense.

▶ **Evangelists**—(Ephesians 4:11)—The ability to clearly communicate the message of salvation through Christ. The person also has a great burden for lost people and a consuming desire to see people won to Christ, even more so than the average believer, and is effective in seeing people become believers.

▶ **Pastor-Teacher**—(Ephesians 4:11)—The only dual gift in the New Testament. A pastor-teacher is one who shepherds the church by feeding and nourishing it with the Word of God. He also guards and protects the flock (Acts 20:31).

▶ **Teacher**—(Romans 12:7; I Corinthians 12:28)—The God-given ability to explain God's Word to people. Sometimes this gift is given along with the gift of pastor (see above). The person with this gift will have a deep desire to study the Bible and to communicate it to others in a way that benefits them. This is an important gift in that it is mentioned in three of the five lists. The teaching gift is one that can be developed and matured with time and evaluation.

▶ **Encouraging**—(Romans 12:8)—The word "encouragement" means to call to one's side to help. And this gift has two built-in ideas: (1) to console or comfort someone, and (2) to drive home spiritual truth. In other words, it can put its arms around you or it can give you a boost in the pants! Some translations call this the gift of exhortation. The person with this gift enjoys building up and cheering on others with his or her words.

SERVING GIFTS—Involve the strong desire to help others through the giving of time, talents, or treasure.

▶ **Giving**—(Romans 12:8)—Present when a person joyfully and sacrificially gives out of his or her finances to meet the needs of others. This is done without desire for recognition; does not require one to be wealthy (Philippians 4:10-16).

▶ **Leading (Administration)**—(Romans 12:8)—Also translated as the gift of ruling. This person has the ability to organize and manage the affairs of ministry in the church. This person enjoys taking a project and seeing it to completion.

▶ **Showing Mercy**—(Romans 12:8)—A burden to reach out and minister to those who are in real need, such as the poor, the homeless, and the destitute.

▶ **Helps (Serving)**—(Romans 12:7)—The gift of helps involves a desire to serve others whenever and wherever you're needed. Usually this person is a behind-the-scenes worker.

1. Now go back and circle all the gifts that you think you might have.

Of course, in addition to the spiritual gifts that God has given to us as believers, we are to use our natural skills, talents, and abilities for God as well.

2. What skills, talents, or abilities do you have that you can use for God?

KEEP In Mind

How do you go about discovering which gift you have? And how do you find out how to use it to serve the body of Christ?

Here are six ideas to get you started:

PRAY—Spend time in prayer telling God how you want to serve Him and His people. Ask Him to show you what your gift is (James 1:5; Matthew 7:7-11).

STUDY—Look up passages mentioned earlier. Select a gift and find out how it was exercised in the New Testament. Study again the explanations given in this chapter. You may even want to buy a book on spiritual gifts.

DESIRE—What spiritual activity do you really want to do? What do you really enjoy doing? What gives you joy and satisfaction as you do it? As you continue to submit your heart to God in prayer and study, He will put His desires for you in your heart (Psalm 37:4; Proverbs 3:5, 6; I Timothy 3:1). That's a promise!

ABILITY—What do you do best? What are you good at doing? In what areas do you feel you are already spiritually gifted? What are you doing now that could be related to a spiritual gift?

CONFIRMATION—What gift do others see in you? Do they see what you see? Try choosing three or four godly, mature believers who know God and know you. Ask them, "Do you see any areas of giftedness in me? If so, out of all the gifts, which one do you believe I might have?" If others are seeing what you're discovering through prayer, study, desire, and ability, you can be almost certain that is your gift.

BLESSING—In what area of service does God seem to be blessing you? In what ways has God used you in the past to meet people's needs? Where have you seen spiritual fruit? If you haven't had the chance to find this out yet, then volunteer to serve in some area of ministry where you think you might be good.

Remember, even though you already have a gift, the discovery of that gift may take a little time. But be patient and give God time to develop your gift. Once you find out what your gift is, use it to serve the body of Christ. Serve in God's strength, not merely your own (I Peter 4:11). Develop it through further study and invite others' feedback on how you can improve your spiritual service.

Don't be jealous of others' gifts. God has designed the body with great diversity. Out of that diversity comes harmony and unity (I Corinthians 12:1-30). See yourself as a player on a team—you play a certain position, not every position. Just play your position well.

So what about John, the piano player? What encouragement could we give to him? Looking back, what spiritual gift do you think John might have and why?

Any skill or talent can be used for spiritual purposes. In other words, you can use Your talents to serve the Lord. But don't forget the spiritual gift God has given you.

PRAY About It

Spend time in prayer focusing on the questions asked in the "Keep In Mind" section. Ask God to guide you in your search. Talk frankly with Him about any of the spiritual gifts you circled. Pray about this long term. Keep a record of your prayers and answers concerning this.

WEEK ‹15› Apples, Oranges, and Disciples

The Fruit of the Spirit

1 Don't Let Discouragement Get You Down

Discouragement has been called the greatest and most powerful weapon of the devil. It can come out of nowhere, leaving you depressed, unmotivated, and dejected. It can dampen your spirit, dishearten you, and perhaps even destroy you. One of the deadlier results of discouragement is that it steals your hope. And without hope, you become like a deflated balloon—without the power or the will to carry on. Although discouragement is a tough obstacle, it can be overcome. Consider the following examples:

• A Munich schoolmaster once told Albert Einstein that he would never amount to much.

• Decca Recording Company turned down a new group, stating, "We don't like their sound. Groups of guitars are on their way out." The group's name? The Beatles.

• Around the turn of the century, a man named Simon Newcomb said, "Flight by machines heavier than air is unpractical and insignificant . . . utterly impossible."

• Michael Jordan, perhaps the greatest basketball player of all time, was cut from his high school basketball team as a sophomore.

• A man named John Hunt (1775-1848) once said, "Rembrandt is not to be compared in the painting of character with our extraordinarily gifted artist Mr. Rippingdale." Mr. Ripping . . . who?

• A Kansas City newspaper turned down the application of a young artist, saying he had no talent. He returned to his mice-infested garage to keep drawing. One night, he spotted one of the little mice playing in the corner. He picked up his pencil and started sketching—and Mickey Mouse was born! Walt Disney didn't believe the lie of discouragement.

As a Christian, some of the biggest and best lies you will ever hear go something like this:

"You will never be like Christ. You're worthless. How can you call yourself a Christian? Look at your failures. God doesn't love you. Look at how many times you've let the Lord down. You can't live like Jesus in a world like this. Why even try? It's a hopeless cause. You're a hopeless cause! Give up. Go back to the way you were. Admit you just can't make it as a follower of Christ."

Have you ever heard lies like that? If so, you need to know that these dark, depressing thoughts come from the devil. They can also come from other people or your own heart. The important thing to remember is: don't believe these discouraging lies.

On the other hand, here's some encouraging truth to believe in:

• You can produce spiritual character with God's help.

• You can bear the fruit of the Spirit.

• You can be like Jesus.

This chapter can give you hope by helping you understand what the fruit of the Spirit is, and how you can bear that fruit in your life.

2 God's Produce Section

1. The fruit of the Spirit comes in several different forms. Try to unscramble the following kinds of fruits listed below to see what kind of fruit you can bear.

["Egg"ception: If your un"scrambling" efforts leave you feeling "fried," don't let the stress "boil" you over. Instead, feel free to look up the verses to help make this section "over easy." (If you do figure out the words without checking out the verses, read the verses anyway.)]

The fruit of (e a s p i r) _____ (Hebrews 13:15).

The fruit of (d o g o   r w o s k) _____ (Colossians 1:10).

The fruit of (w n e   r a h i c s s n t i) _____ (Romans 1:13).

The fruit of (e h t   i p t s i r) _____ (Galatians 5:22).

2. According to John 15:2, 5, what can you discover about God's will for you in this area of bearing fruit?

3. What will be the result (John 15:8)?

4. Why do you think bearing fruit glorifies God?

When fruit appears in our lives, it gives evidence of the fact that we are Christ's disciples. Take a look at what this fruit looks like in our everyday lives.

3 Fresh Fruit—Three Kinds

Perhaps the fruit of the Spirit is the greatest benefit of the Holy Spirit at work because it deals with our character. The Holy Spirit is committed to building godly character in you. One way He does this is by producing fruit in you.

In Galatians 5:22, Paul refers to these nine character qualities as the fruit of the Spirit instead of fruits. This is because when you get the Spirit, you get the source of all the fruit. So think of this fruit, not as nine different fruits—like a banana, an orange, an apple, etc.—but think of them as the same kind of fruit, like a cluster of grapes.

1. In Galatians 5:16-21, what does Paul contrast the fruit of the Spirit with?

Notice the fruit that is identified. These are the results of a life controlled by the flesh, not the Spirit. Like a thermometer, you can read your spiritual temperature by looking at the fruit of your life. When you walk by the Spirit, a whole new crop appears! Think of a grapevine when you think about growing as a Christian. As you watch the vine grow, you notice there is fruit growing on it.

Examine this spiritual fruit one by one, and get a quick glance at what each one means.

LOVE (I Corinthians 13:4-8, 13)—

2. Love is . . .

3. How does a Christian demonstrate this love (I John 4:20, 21)?

4. Why do you think this is such a good test of our love for God?

5. Can you think of one person you are having a tough time loving? What part of your definition above do you need to work on?

We need to remind ourselves that love didn't originate in Hollywood, or in soap operas or love songs. Love was born in the heart of God and is poured out in our hearts by the Holy Spirit (Romans 5:5). Love is not just an emotion. It involves a choice. And it's the Holy Spirit's job to give you love for all people, whether they are easy or difficult to love. God provides the strength to choose to love, even when you don't feel like it.

JOY—The Bible says the joy God offers is full (John 16:14), overflowing (I Peter 1:8), complete (I John 1:4), commanded (Philippians 4:4), and not based on circumstances (Hebrews 12:2). It comes from a strong relationship with Christ. The greater the relationship, the greater the joy! And though joy can be emotional, it doesn't always have to be.

6. Christian joy is a deep, abiding contentment. It's a strong undercurrent of happiness—but a happiness of a different kind. What normally comes to mind when you think of joy?

7. What, in your opinion, is the difference between joy and happiness?

8. What is the surest way to have this joy (John 15:10, 11)?

PEACE—There is a lot of talk about peace these days, probably because there is so little of it! But no one has the kind of peace Christians have access to. The Bible says you already have peace with God (Romans 5:1) through Christ's death. But you can also experience the peace of God every day!

9. Describe this incredible peace from the verses below:

Philippians 4:7

John 14:27

Isaiah 26:3

10. Can you think of certain circumstances that tend to rob you of your peace? How can the verses above help you in those times?

4 More Fresh Fruit—Three More Kinds

PATIENCE—Biblical patience goes much deeper than just waiting for something or someone. The fruit of patience means to endure tough times and tough people. It means to be slow to anger and to hang in there. To be patient means to be understanding with the faults and shortcomings of others (Colossians 3:12; II Timothy 4:2). Patience doesn't seek revenge, but shows love instead (I Corinthians 13:4). And that's something only the Holy Spirit can produce in us! It's unlike the man who prayed, "Lord, give me patience . . . and give it to me now!"

1. In what way has the Lord been patient with you? How do you need to demonstrate the same patience with others?

KINDNESS—This character quality means you treat others with tenderness and gentleness. Every Christian should be a kind person (Ephesians 4:32; Colossians 3:12). Unfortunately, this particular fruit has become a little rotten in some believers' lives.

2. Why do you think Christians need kindness now more than ever?

3. What is one way you can allow the Spirit to produce kindness in you (Ephesians 4:31)?

4. How is the Spirit affected when we are unkind to one another (Ephesians 4:30)?

GOODNESS—This word refers to being morally upright, both our character and our actions. It refers to having a pure heart, but also suggests we do good to others.

5. What are four practical ways you can showcase this fruit in your life?

    1. _____ (Philippians 4:8, 9)

    2. _____ (III John 11)

    3. _____ (Luke 6:32-35)

    4. _____ (Galatians 6:10)

5 More Fresh Fruit— Three More Kinds

FAITHFULNESS—To be loyal, reliable, dependable, or trustworthy. When this fruit is evident, others can trust you and put their confidence in you. We all know God can be trusted because of His never-ending faithfulness to us (Isaiah 25:1; Lamentations 3:23), but in what way are you to be faithful to Him? How is God depending on you (II Corinthians 5:18; II Timothy 2:2)?

1. In what areas is God looking for you to be faithful (Matthew 25:21)?

2. What does Jesus promise in this verse to the one who is faithful?

Faithfulness honors God, and God honors faithfulness.

GENTLENESS—What does it mean to be gentle? Is a gentle person some soupy, spineless individual who gives in to everyone and everything? Is it something only girls can have but real men don't? Not quite. Gentleness involves placing yourself in a position of humility, of serving someone in a kind manner. It means you handle people as if they were fragile pieces of glass . . . gently.

3. How does Paul picture this in I Thessalonians 2:7?

4. How could you go about pursuing gentleness?

SELF-CONTROL—This fruit refers to restraining your desires. Like an athlete, you exercise discipline over your mind, body, and heart, keeping yourself under control. It's the idea of being able to consistently say no to wrong desires and yes to the things you know are right.

5. In what areas do you need more self-control?

____ eating habits   ____ choosing friends

____ date life   ____ laziness

____ lust   ____ keeping priorities straight

____ homework   ____ thought life

____ spending your money   ____ how you spend your time

____ attitude toward parents   ____ anger, temper

____ your speech   ____ other

6. Which of these are more difficult for you?

7. How would your lack of self-control in these areas affect others?

8. What is Paul's advice to you here (I Corinthians 9:24-27)?

9. What do you think Paul meant by "strict training . . . beat my body . . . make it my slave"?

10. What does God promise the one who has self-control (I Corinthians 9:25)?

KEEP In Mind

You might be wondering at this point, Is something wrong with me if the fruit of the Spirit aren't real evident in my life? Great question!

And God's Word has the answer, right there in this same chapter (Galatians 5). Paul gives two simple perspectives on how to get rid of the desires of your sinful nature and how to allow the Spirit to produce His fruit in you. His key ideas are in verses 16 and 25.

Read Galatians 5 a few times and underline what you think are key phrases concerning living by the Spirit. Circle specific ways to live. Cross out specific things Scripture says to avoid. Create goals for personal growth based on Galatians 5.

Remember, don't worry about trying to produce this fruit in your life. That's His job. It's His fruit. You don't ever hear orange trees grunting to try and pop out oranges on their branches. Of course not. Orange trees live like orange trees, and in time produce oranges! So live for Jesus and follow Him. That doesn't mean you shouldn't ever focus in on a particular character trait and work on it. You should. But your part is to follow and obey. His part is to produce.

Don't be discouraged when you're not growing in a certain area as fast as you'd like to be. God is committed to you (Philippians 1:6). And He is at work in you and for you, even when you don't realize it and can't see it (Romans 8:28; Philippians 2:13). And as you keep growing in these areas, your life will bring glory to God (John 15:8).

As you complete this book, take heart in knowing God is committed to you. He loves you so much. And He will never give up on you. That is why, with Jesus, you're *Never the Same!*

PRAY About It

Just because this is the last "Pray About It" section in this book, doesn't mean you have to stop praying. Don't give up on this vital area. Keep your communication lines open with God. A really good way to do that is to keep a written record of your prayer requests and answers; so keep going!

This final page is for you to write about what's going on in your life right now—things to praise God for, things to ask God, things to thank Him for. Take a few minutes today to thank God for pouring out His grace on you and for making Himself accessible to you.

God, thank You for . . .